# Saddam Hussein

**Other books in the Heroes and Villains series include:**

Al Capone
Frederick Douglass
Adolf Hitler
Martin Luther King Jr.
Oskar Schindler

Heroes and Villains

# Saddam Hussein

Gail B. Stewart

LUCENT
BOOKS®

THOMSON

GALE

San Diego • Detroit • New York • San Francisco • Cleveland • New Haven. Conn. • Waterville. Maine • London • Munich

© 2004 by Lucent Books. Lucent Books is an imprint of The Gale Group, Inc.,
a division of Thomson Learning, Inc.

Lucent Books® and Thomson Learning™ are trademarks used herein under license.

*For more information, contact*
Lucent Books
27500 Drake Rd.
Farmington Hills, MI 48331-3535
Or you can visit our Internet site at http://www.gale.com

**LIBRARY OF CONGRESS CATALOGING-IN-PUBLICATION DATA**

Stewart, Gail, 1949–
    Saddam Hussein / by Gail B. Stewart.
       p. cm. — (Heroes and villains series)
Summary: A biography of the deposed president of Iraq, discussing his early years,
education, religious fervor and hatred of non-Islamic societies, his brutal rule of Iraq,
and the uncertainty of his fate after the United States military attacks in 2003.
Includes bibliographical references and index.
    ISBN 1-59018-350-9
    1. Hussein, Saddam, 1937—Juvenile literature. 2. Presidents—Iraq—Biography—
Juvenile literature. [1. Hussein, Saddam, 1937- 2. Presidents—Iraq.] I. Title. II. Series.
    DS79.66.H87S77 2004b
    956.7044'092—dc22

                                                 2003015619

Printed in the United States of America

# Contents

FOREWORD                                    6

INTRODUCTION
The Secret Graves                           8

CHAPTER 1
"Son of the Alleys"                        12

CHAPTER 2
Saddam the Baathist                        20

CHAPTER 3
Saddam the Killer                          30

CHAPTER 4
Saddam the President                       43

CHAPTER 5
A New Path to War                          55

CHAPTER 6
Saddam Surviving                           68

Notes                                      83
For Further Reading                        87
Works Consulted                            88
Index                                      90
Picture Credits                            95
About the Author                           96

Good and evil are an ever-present feature of human history. Their presence is reflected through the ages in tales of great heroism and extraordinary villainy. Such tales provide insight into human nature, whether they involve two people or two thousand, for the essence of heroism and villainy is found in deeds rather than in numbers. It is the deeds that pique our interest and lead us to wonder what prompts a man or woman to perform such acts.

Samuel Johnson, the eminent eighteenth-century English writer, once wrote, "The two great movers of the human mind are the desire for good, and fear of evil." The pairing of desire and fear, possibly two of the strongest human emotions, helps explain the intense fascination people have with all things good and evil— and by extension, heroic and villainous.

People are attracted to the person who reaches into a raging river to pull a child from what could have been a watery grave for both, and to the person who risks his or her own life to shepherd hundreds of desperate black slaves to safety on the Underground Railroad. We wonder what qualities these heroes possess that enable them to act against self-interest, and even their own survival. We also wonder if, under similar circumstances, we would behave as they do.

Evil, on the other hand, horrifies as well as intrigues us. Few people can look upon the drifter who mutilates and kills a neighbor or the dictator who presides over the torture and murder of thousands of his own citizens without feeling a sense of revulsion. And yet, as Joseph Conrad writes, we experience "the fascination of the abomination." How else to explain the overwhelming success of a book such as Truman Capote's *In Cold Blood*, which examines in horrifying detail a vicious and senseless murder that took place in the American heartland in the 1960s? The popularity of murder mysteries and Court TV are also evidence of the human fascination with villainy.

Most people recoil in the face of such evil. Yet most feel a deep-seated curiosity about the kind of person who could commit a terrible act. It is perhaps a reflection of our innermost fears that we wonder whether we could resist or stand up to such behavior in our presence or even if we ourselves possess the capacity to commit such terrible crimes.

The Lucent Books Heroes and Villains series capitalizes on our fascination with the perpetrators of both good and evil by introducing readers to some of history's most revered heroes and hated villains. These include heroes such as Frederick Douglass, who knew firsthand the humiliation of slavery and, at great risk to himself, publicly fought to abolish the institution of slavery in America. It also includes villains such as Adolf Hitler, who is remembered both for the devastation of Europe and for the murder of 6 million Jews and thousands of Gypsies, Slavs, and others whom Hitler deemed unworthy of life.

Each book in the Heroes and Villains series examines the life story of a hero or villain from history. Generous use of primary and secondary source quotations gives readers eyewitness views of the life and times of each individual as well as enlivens the narrative. Notes and annotated bibliographies provide stepping-stones to further research.

# THE SECRET GRAVES

Two men signal the backhoe into position on the abandoned soccer field. The backhoe chugs and squeaks noisily as it begins to dig up the weeds and dirt. About a dozen men stand near the hole, watching carefully. Suddenly, one of the men yells, and the forklift driver stops. The men talk to the driver, who then resumes digging—but more slowly. As the forklift overturns the soil, there is a flash of white, as two skulls are unearthed. Then a jumble of bones surface—some with bits of clothing or flesh still attached—and the men carefully place the remains into bags.

It is another of Iraq's mass graves, containing between five and ten thousand bodies. At least ten others have been discovered in cities such as Basra, Babylon, and Baghdad, and some human rights organizations are certain that there are hundreds more scattered throughout the country.

## "My Son Was No Criminal"

When Saddam Hussein's government fell in the U.S.-led attack in March 2003, large numbers of secret files were found in his party headquarters. An astonishing eighteen tons of paper—more than 5 million pages—convey information on the systematic torture, murder, and disposal of Iraqi citizens by Saddam's own executioners. It is believed that during Saddam's twenty-four years as leader of Iraq, as many as three hundred thousand Iraqis were murdered and thrown into these mass graves.

Until the fall of the Iraqi government, families of the victims were unsure of the fate of their loved ones, although many suspected the worst. Some were killed because they had been openly critical of Saddam's government. Others because they were Shiites, a different sect of Islam than Saddam. Some were accused of associating with Shiites, or with those of a different political party.

Some were killed for reasons which are a mystery to their loved ones. Dawad, a twenty-one-year old construction worker, went to work one day and never came home. His family was bewildered. Did he say something to the wrong person, or tell a joke that might be construed as critical of Saddam? No one could guess. "My son was no criminal, never talked about politics or religion," says Salima, his mother. "He hated Saddam, but he was quiet about it."[1]

## Mountains of Files

Dawad's body is probably contained in one of the mass graves, but finding and identifying it will be difficult. The Committee of Free Prisoners, a volunteer group, is working with the mountains of Saddam's files, but the process is tedious

An Iraqi man views photos of people who disappeared during Saddam Hussein's regime.

A volunteer with the Committee of Free Prisoners sorts through Saddam Hussein's secret files to help identify bodies in mass graves.

and very slow. After six weeks, the names of five thousand executed prisoners have been posted on the wall outside their offices, and every Saturday, more names are posted. Crowds of people cluster around the list, hoping that they will find news of a relative or friend that has been missing.

Rather than wait for a list, many people go to a mass grave when it is opened. They search through the bones, hoping to see something—false teeth, a wooden leg—anything that could identify their loved ones. One man found his brother by noticing the chipped front tooth of a skull. One of the dead was identified

because of a scrap of a shirt that clung to his bones. A man found his wife—not because of her remains, but because their two small daughters had been shot, too, and buried on top of her.

For years no one knew that the graves were there, except the executioners and those in Iraqi intelligence. To keep dogs from digging up the graves, many of the graves had been guarded by thousands of erect hypodermic needles, just under the top layer of dirt. Now, however, the files are no longer secret, and the graves are being opened one by one. "We would never have had the courage to do this when Saddam was alive," notes one Iraqi taxi driver, searching for his cousins. "If I had tried this a few weeks ago, I might be lying here, too."[2]

## The Legacy of Saddam

While gathering and sorting through piles of bones is a grisly process, people who have missing loved ones are intent on finding them. Islamic law stresses that a proper burial is essential, and the mass graves are far from proper. It is crucial, say worried family members, that they have at least part of a body to bury.

The sobbing families and the tons of paper documenting the torture and execution of Iraqi people is the legacy of Saddam Hussein. As of July 2003, Saddam has not been seen since the fall of his government. One thing is certain, however. The death and destruction that he caused during his presidency will ensure that his name is not forgotten.

## Chapter One

# "SON OF THE ALLEYS"

The man who became the most feared and powerful man in Iraq began his life in a squalid little village called Al-Ouja, near the town of Tikrit, about one hundred miles north of Baghdad. There were only fifteen or twenty families in Al-Ouja, and they all lived in windowless huts made of mud bricks. There were no paved roads, electricity, or running water; when the weather was cold, people burned dried cow dung. Saddam recalled years later, "Life was very difficult everywhere in Iraq. Very few people wore shoes, and in many cases they only wore them on special occasions. Some peasants would not put on their shoes until they had reached their destination so that they would look smart."[3]

There was no school in the village, and almost no one in Al-Ouja could read or write. A few families sent children to school in Tikrit, but most preferred to have their children at home to help with work. Some villagers raised fruits and vegetables, but the majority made their living as smugglers and pirates. In Arabic, *Al-Ouja* means "the turning," named after the sharp bend the Tigris River makes near the town and that bend provided opportunity for crime. The slow-moving boats traveling the river often became mired in the mud near Al-Ouja, and villagers were usually waiting to loot the cargo and sell it later.

## "To Clash"

Saddam was born on April 28, 1937, and at that time, it was the custom for a father to name his children. Saddam's father died, either before his son was born or soon afterward, and the job fell to Saddam's uncle Khairallah. Khairallah decided on Saddam, which means "to clash" or "to strike" in Arabic. According to custom, the baby was given his father's first name—Hussein—as his last name.

Saddam's mother, Subha, was a fortune-teller in Al-Ouja. She wore long black dresses with pockets filled with shells and stones, which she used in her predictions. She was a heavyset, sullen woman, who had the blue-black tattoos on her chin, cheeks, and forehead which were traditional to many young Arab women at that time.

Subha was concerned that she could not afford to raise the child on her own. Her brother Khairallah, serving in the Iraqi army and stationed at the nearby town of Tikrit, agreed that Saddam could live in his home until Subha was able to support herself. The boy remained with Khairallah only until he was six, however, for in 1941, Khairallah was arrested for taking part in a rebellion against the government. Saddam went back to Al-Ouja to live with his mother and her new husband.

## "The Lowest of the Low"

Subha's second husband was Hassan al-Ibrahim, one of her first cousins; marrying cousins was fairly common in Iraq at that time. Hassan had been married already, and though Islamic law allowed a man up to four wives, Subha insisted that he divorce his first wife before marrying her.

Those who knew the family said that marrying Hassan was a large step down for Subha. His family, known as the

Ibrahim clan, was well known for thievery, and even in a village where crime was a way of life, Ibrahims were not trusted. "[Saddam's father's clan] had a bad reputation," recalled one neighbor, "but the Ibrahims were even worse . . . [they were] the lowest of the low. Everyone in the area hated them."[4]

If Saddam had expected to be welcomed by his stepfather, he was sadly

Saddam Hussein and his family pose in front of the clay hut where he was born.

mistaken. Hassan, who had worked for a short time as a school janitor in Tikrit but was now unemployed, made it very clear that the boy was unwanted. He woke Saddam each morning at dawn by screaming, "Get up, you son of a whore. Go tend the sheep."[5] He was critical of Saddam, and often beat him on the legs and backside with a stick coated with asphalt.

Subha did little to defend her son, reportedly encouraging him to help earn money for the family by stealing sheep and chickens from nearby farms. One who knew the family well during those years recalled that the family would steal and divide the spoils the same night. "Saddam's mother used to preside over the division of the loot—wheat or rye, sheep, maybe a few pieces of gold and silver."[6]

## No Friends

One biographer notes that during this period of his life, Saddam was known by villagers as a *ibn aziqa*, or "son of the alleys."[7] Left to fend for himself much of the time, he developed the cunningness and skill to survive the volatile temper of his stepfather and the apparent disinter-

## Arab Birthdays

*Traditionally, Arabs in the Middle East have never celebrated their birthdays. As biographer Con Coughlin explains in his book* Saddam: King of Terror, *Saddam Hussein's birthdate has often been the subject of much controversy because of this tradition:*

Officially, Saddam was born on April 28, 1937, and, to lend the date authenticity, in 1980 Saddam made it a national holiday. Given the primitive nature of Iraqi society at the time of his birth, it is, perhaps, hardly surprising that this date has been challenged on several occasions, with some of his contemporaries arguing that he was born a good couple of years earlier, in 1935, while other commentators have claimed that he was born as late as 1939. This might be explained by the fact that the whole process for registering births, marriages, and deaths was exceedingly primitive. At this time it was the custom for the authorities to give all peasant children the nominal birth date of July 1; it was only the year that they attempted to get right. This would certainly explain why a certificate presented in one of Saddam's official biographies gives July 1, 1939, as the date of his birth. In fact, Saddam acquired his official birthdate from his friend and future co-conspirator, Abdul Karim al-Shaikhly, who came from a well-established Baghdad family and so had the advantage of possessing an authentic birthdate. [Coughlin quotes one contemporary of Saddam's as saying,] "Saddam was always jealous of Karim for knowing his own birthday. So Saddam simply copied it for himself."

est of his mother. He was not as fortunate with other children his age, however. Because of the bad reputation of his stepfather, Saddam was looked down on by local boys. To protect himself from their attacks, he would carry an iron bar, and he was not afraid to use it.

People who knew Saddam when he was young say that he used the iron bar for more than protection. When bored, he sometimes heated the bar on the fire and when it was red-hot, stabbed a sheep or other animal in the belly, just to watch the animal suffer. But while he could be unspeakably cruel in some of his dealings with animals, he recalled years later that the dearest friend he had as a young boy was his horse. "A relationship between man and animal," he explained, "can at times be more affectionate, intimate, and unselfish than relations between two human beings."[8] So much did he love the horse, he said, that when he learned about the animal's death, his hand became paralyzed for more than a week—a sign of grief, he believed.

## Desiring an Education

Saddam had not thought much about school, since the poorest villagers never sent their children to Tikrit. On the few occasions that he saw his young cousin Adnan, however, he began considering an education. Adnan was younger, but was already learning to draw, read, and write in his elementary school. Saddam approached his stepfather about going to school, but the answer was an emphatic no.

In 1947, however, Saddam ran away from his family in Al-Ouja to Tikrit. His uncle Khairallah had been released from prison and was now teaching school in the town. Determined to start school and live with Khairallah, Saddam appealed to some relatives nearby his home in Al-Ouja, and they provided him with transportation and even a pistol, for protection. His journey was successful, and soon after arriving in Tikrit, he joined his cousin Adnan at school.

Saddam's education did not start well, for he was far behind most of the other students. Though ten years old, Saddam was placed in a class of five-year-olds, and even then he struggled. He was the only one in his class who could not write his own name, which humilated him. Sometimes to deflect the jokes and ridicule of his fellow students, Saddam became a class clown. A favorite trick was pretending to embrace his teacher, while slipping a live snake in the man's robes.

## Hoping for a Military Career

Saddam's cousin Adnan proved to be a good friend, helping Saddam with schoolwork and encouraging him to keep trying even though the work was difficult. He continued to struggle with reading, although his teachers agreed that he had an astonishing memory for even the smallest details. When he was sixteen, Saddam graduated from the primary school at Tikrit, which is approximately the same as an eighth grade education in the United States.

While Saddam had had difficulty in primary school, he was anxious to continue his education further. His goal, not surprisingly, was to be an army officer like Khairallah had been. To serve as an officer, one must attend the Baghdad Military Academy, a very prestigious school with rigorous entrance requirements. The entrance exam proved to be too difficult for Saddam, however, and he was rejected. With no other goals in mind, he halfheartedly agreed to accompany Khairallah and Adnan to Baghdad, the capital, where his uncle had a teaching post at a new school.

Saddam's high school years, say historians, proved to be extremely important in forming his views on Iraq's place in the world and its relationships with the West. Almost immediately when he began high school in 1955, he knew history was going to be his favorite subject.

## An Ancient Empire

Although he had learned about the geography of Iraq in primary school, he was completely unaware of the rich history of his native land. He learned that the land which was now Iraq was called *Rafidain*—meaning "between rivers"—because of the Tigris and Euphrates Rivers that surround it. (Later, the Greeks called the region "Mesopotamia," with the same meaning.) *Rafidain* had been the site of the first civilizations on the planet. The region between the Tigris and Euphrates Rivers is often described as "the cradle of civilization," because of evidence discovered by anthropologists that shows the area was inhabited ten thousand years ago.

In the seventh century, the Arab people established the first Islamic Empire in Mesopotamia. It was first ruled by the prophet Muhammad, and later by his successors, who were known as caliphs. Over the centuries, the Islamic Empire expanded to include territory from North Africa to Central Asia and Western European nations, such as Spain. During the years of the Islamic Empire, beginning around A.D. 632, the Muslim philosophers, scholars, and artists were among the world's best.

In addition to learning about the glories of his homeland, Saddam learned about the factions that had split the empire. When Muhammad died in A.D. 632, there was disagreement about who should become his successor. One group, known as the Sunnis, believed strongly that Muhammad's successor must be chosen by finding the wisest and most devout of his supporters. The Sunnis chose Abu Bakr, a close friend of Muhammad, as the caliph when Muhammad died.

The other faction, known as Shiites, believed that one could only be a caliph if he were a blood relative of Muhammad. The Shiites supported Ali, a cousin of Muhammad, as the caliph. The quarrel over something so basic about the Islamic faith produced a sharp division between the two sides, which has continued to modern times in Islamic countries.

A mural depicts Saddam Hussein as part of Iraq's rich history. The country is known as "the cradle of civilization".

## Changing Hands

In the early 1700s, the region was so fragmented that it was easily taken over by the Turks of the Ottoman Empire. The Turks did not differentiate between the very different regions of the Islamic Empire; it was simply a large parcel of land that was now under Turkish control. They established governors in the larger cities, such as Baghdad, but because the Turks were not a presence in the rural areas, they had no power there. In those areas, the sheikhs or tribal leaders were in charge, just as they had been for centuries.

The power shifted for Iraq again in 1917 during World War I. For the first time, the British became involved in the region. Hoping to break the stranglehold the Turks had throughout the Middle East, British diplomats held secret talks with Arab leaders and learned that the Arabs were hoping to be rid of the Turks, too. An alliance was forged between the British and the Arabs—if the Arabs would help the British fight the Turks, the British would grant the region total independence.

The Arab uprisings destabilized the region, and the British were able to take over Iraq. The British government did

# Iraq's British-Drawn Borders

For many Iraqis, one of the most hated results of the British domination of their country was the way the borders were created. When the British took control of the region in 1920, it combined three former Ottoman provinces—Baghdad, Mosul, and Basra. When the British decided on the borders for Iraq, however, they seemed to ignore the effects of those borders on the people of the new nation.

The northern border ran through a mountainous area inhabited by the Kurds, a non-Arab people. The British had earlier promised the Kurds their own homeland, but had reneged on the promise. Instead, the British divided the region where the Kurds lived among Russia, Iran, Iraq, and Turkey. The presence of the Kurds has been a problem for those countries and for the regime of Saddam Hussein because they are not Arab.

The southern border was problematic, too. The nation of Kuwait also had been promised more territory by the British—but after World War I, this promise was broken. Britain appeased the Kuwaitis by giving them some of the coastline of Iraq. This proved disastrous for Iraq, which was left with only sixteen miles of coastline—and much of that swampy and shallow. Not surprisingly, the people of Iraq were resentful of what they viewed as unfair treatment at the hands of the British mapmakers.

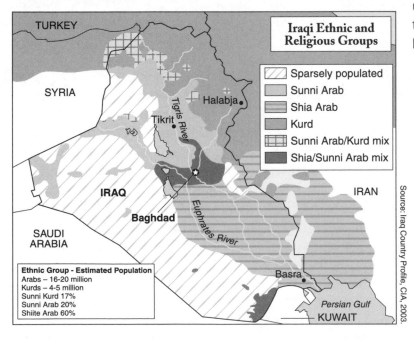

**Iraqi Ethnic and Religious Groups**

- Sparsely populated
- Sunni Arab
- Shia Arab
- Kurd
- Sunni Arab/Kurd mix
- Shia/Sunni Arab mix

**Ethnic Group - Estimated Population**
Arabs – 16-20 million
Kurds – 4-5 million
Sunni Kurd 17%
Sunni Arab 20%
Shiite Arab 60%

TURKEY
SYRIA
Halabja
Tikrit
Tigris River
IRAQ
Baghdad
Euphrates River
SAUDI ARABIA
Basra
IRAN
Persian Gulf
KUWAIT

Source: Iraq Country Profile, CIA, 2003.

not keep its promise to the Arabs, however. After World War I, at the San Remo peace conference in Italy, it was decided by the nations in attendance that Britain should be given a mandate to govern the region. The Arab people living in the region objected and reminded the British that they had promised freedom. The British believed that the area was not ready to be independent; the various factions created such instability that any government by the Arab people would be doomed to failure.

## Rebellion

In his studies, Saddam learned that there had been attempts by Iraqi nationalists to drive the British out of Iraq. In each case, however, the British had put down rebellions. The anger that continued to fester among the Iraqis—and especially about the British-controlled monarchy—was evident in Khairallah and many other Iraqi nationalists at the time when Saddam came to Baghdad to begin high school. At the school where he taught, Khairallah was known as a very angry, no-nonsense teacher, who was extremely frank about his views of the government. Years later, one of his students described Khairallah as "a very tough man, a Nazi and a Fascist. All the pupils were in awe of him, both because of his record in fighting the British and because of his political views."[9]

Khairallah was very pleased that Saddam was taking an interest in Iraq's history, and in its current events. Saddam and his uncle often talked for hours about how the Iraqi people had been mistreated by the British, and how the Middle East would be far better off without the influence of Western powers. Saddam was in awe of his uncle, not only for the knowledge he had of world events, but because of Khairallah's own part in a revolution against the government years before, in 1941.

Saddam's overwhelming interest in Iraq's history did not carry over to his other classes, however. He had never been a good student, but at this time he became impatient and irritated with class discussions, and he mocked the idea that independence could be won by political means. Results, he often told others, could only be attained by force.

That idea was one he lived by even as a teenager. At one point during his high school years, the headmaster intended to expel Saddam because of his unruly behavior and poor grades. "When Saddam heard about this decision," said a fellow student years later, "he came to his headmaster's room and threatened him with death. He said: 'I will kill you if you do not withdraw your threat against me to expel me from the school.'"[10] Certain that the teenager was serious, the headmaster changed his mind and allowed Saddam to stay in school. It was not that Saddam really wanted to remain at the school; rather, he simply wanted to leave on his own terms. That time would come very soon, for he was far more interested in what he could learn on the streets of Baghdad.

## Chapter Two

# SADDAM THE BAATHIST

By 1956, the political climate in Baghdad was tense. More and more people were dissatisfied with the British-controlled monarchy, and there was a great deal of talk about the events taking place in another part of the Middle East—Egypt. An Egyptian army officer, Gamal Abdel Nasser, had recently led a rebellion in his country, which had also been living under a monarchy sponsored by Britain. Nasser was a hero to many nationalists in the Middle East, and his success at overthrowing the Egyptian monarchy gave hope that it could be done elsewhere.

## The Baathist Party

Saddam knew that he wanted to be a part of such a change in Iraq, so he stopped attending school. He was far happier sitting in his uncle's house, listening to Khairallah and his friends talk about rebellion and the brilliant future Iraq could have. One of the most interesting of Khairallah's friends was Ahmad Hassan al-Bakr.

Al-Bakr had served in the army with Khairallah, and he was a staunch nationalist. He was one of the leaders of a new political movement called the Baath (meaning "resurrection" or "renaissance") Party. Unlike other political groups in the Middle East at that time, the Baathists were secular, not religious. The Baath Party had begun in the 1940s in Syria, the combined efforts of two schoolteachers, a Christian and a Muslim. They believed that the Middle East could never be free as long as outsiders were controlling their politics and their economies.

Al-Bakr and other Baathists believed strongly that the people of the Middle

East had to unite and rise up against the Europeans who controlled them, and had to abolish the boundaries that the Europeans had drawn. Without such boundaries, the Middle East could once again be a strong kingdom.

Al-Bakr explained to Saddam that unlike other movements in the Middle East, the Baath Party is based not on religion, but ethnicity. Arabs should be brothers, he said, whether they are Christian or Muslim. It is the non-Arabs, he believed, that were causing problems in the region. For example, by establishing arbitrary boundaries in Iraq and other nations, the European powers had mixed Arabs with non-Arabs, such as the Kurds in northern Iraq and the Persians in Iran. Such boundaries, according to al-Bakr, had only made the creation of a true Arab nation more difficult.

## "A Professional Killer"

The Baath Party's message was that change could not occur until the British-controlled monarchy was dismantled—and

British soldiers question an Arab man. Saddam Hussein's Baath Party believed that Arabs could not be free while outsiders controlled their politics and economies.

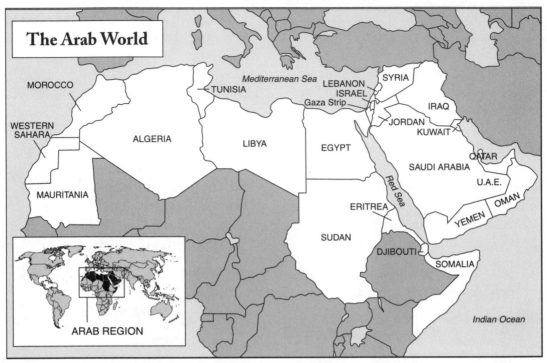

The Arab World

ARAB REGION

the Baathists believed that they were the ones to do that. Saddam was moved by the Baathist message, and he eagerly joined the party in 1957. As one of the youngest members, he was asked to organize a show of force that would impress other young people in Baghdad.

At age twenty and at six foot two, Saddam was strong and imposing and far taller than most Arab men. He roamed the streets, pistol tucked in his shirt, intimidating his former school-mates and organizing street violence to protest the government. Anyone who dared to defend the monarchy or who was foolish enough to criticize the Baathists was beaten up by Saddam and his small gang of followers. Writes biographer Con Coughlin,

Saddam was usually to be found at the forefront of any antigovernment demonstration or riot. In such an environment of perpetual violence and unrest, it was simply a question of time before Saddam killed someone.[11]

It was actually his uncle Khairallah who orchestrated Saddam's first murder. Khairallah was furious with his brother-in-law, a teacher who stood against the Baathist ideals. In 1958, Khairallah ordered Saddam to kill the man, and Saddam eagerly obeyed. As the teacher was walking home from a local coffee shop, Saddam stepped out from behind a tree and shot him dead.

Saddam did not deny the crime to his peers; in fact, he seemed almost proud.

"Saddam told me his uncle gave him a gun and asked him to kill the relative," recalls one man who knew Saddam. "He was a professional killer. But I also have to admit in those days that I admired him. He was brave, courageous, and killed for what he believed in."[12]

## "Blooded"

The police in Tikrit arrested Saddam and Khairallah almost immediately after the murder, and they were jailed. One man who shared a prison cell with them remembers how close Saddam and his uncle were:

> What has stuck in my mind most of all was how Saddam and his uncle kept to themselves in prison. They would choose a far-away corner, away from the rest of the inmates. Despite the small size of the cell in which we were all held, the two of them never gave us a chance to enter into conversation with them.[13]

The man recalls sending another prisoner over to the two to find out the details of their imprisonment, but neither Saddam nor his uncle would say anything.

After six months, however, the police did not have enough evidence to prove that the men had had anything to do with the crime, and they were released. Rather than be horrified that one of their youngest members had committed murder, the Baathist leaders were proud of Saddam. He was considered "blooded," meaning he had killed with honor, and it

would not be long until the twenty-year-old was chosen for an important new assignment, as a reward.

## Bloodshed in the Streets of Baghdad

The monarchy in Iraq had finally fallen in the summer of 1958, but it was not at the hands of the Baath Party. Instead, a group of army officers who were fed up with the government banded together and led armed troops into Baghdad. Calling themselves Free Officers, the group seized control of the palace and shot the young king, Faisal II, and other members of his family.

The Free Officers took control of the radio station, and one of the leaders proclaimed to the city that the Iraqi army had liberated "the beloved homeland from the corrupt crew that imperialism installed."[14] The announcement of the coup, or takeover, caused rioting in the capital's streets. The British embassy was set on fire and many European business representatives were murdered in their hotels. The bodies of the royal family were dragged through the streets as crowds cheered.

Saddam and the other members of the Baath Party cheered, too. They were pleased that the monarchy was gone. The leader of the coup, General Abdul Karim Qassem, had proclaimed himself Iraq's president, and he seemed at first as though he had similar views to the Baathists. He even appointed several Baath Party members to positions in his

King Faisal II's belongings lie in front of the palace after the Free Officers deposed him.

of Western Europe. This plan alarmed the Baathists, who felt that the Soviets would have just as much influence as the British had had before. They maintained that Iraq was an Arab land, and since the Soviets were not Arabs, they should have nothing to do with the way Iraq was governed.

Qassem's government, which at first had had the support of many Iraqis, began to flounder. Violence erupted throughout the country, with Communist Iraqis fighting Arab nationalists. Some of Qassem's fellow Free Officers tried to rebel against him for leaning toward communism, but the coup failed and the men were hanged in the public square in Baghdad, to teach the nationalists a lesson.

new government. In the weeks and months that followed, however, Qassem showed that he was not as interested in creating an all-Arab Middle East as the Baathists had hoped.

## Qassem's Government Attacked

Instead of working exclusively with other Middle Eastern Arab nations, Qassem had a different idea. He wanted to build alliances with the Soviet Union, the enemy

What followed over the next weeks was one of the bloodiest times in Iraq's history. After some nationalists staged an uprising against Qassem in the city of Mosul, Qassem took action. "The communist militias were given a free hand in Mosul to take revenge," notes one historian. "Rapes, murders, lootings, summary trials and executions in front of cheering mobs followed."[15] Realizing that their message of nationalism could put their lives in danger, Saddam and the Baathists did their recruiting more quietly. However, they now had a new goal—the assassination of the new president.

## Snags

The Baathists secretly planned their assassination for the fall of 1959. They chose a six-man hit squad, and Saddam was excited to be among those selected. Up until this time, his party activities had been limited to rabble-rousing in the streets of Baghdad. Although he was still a junior member of the party, Saddam had been hoping for a chance to contribute something far more valuable to the cause of nationalism.

The plan was to ambush Qassem's car as he was driving to or from his office in central Baghdad. They had noticed that he rarely varied his route, and this made preparations easy. One of the Baathists was to drive his car into an intersection and block the street. As Qassem's car stopped, the squad of six men would rush out from behind nearby buildings from both sides of the street. Two were supposed to fire into the front of the car to kill the bodyguard and driver, and two into the back, where Qassem rode. Saddam and another man were to provide cover for the shooters, in case there was return fire. It seemed a fairly simple plan.

October 7, 1959, was chosen as the day Qassem would be assassinated. He was to attend a reception that evening at the East German embassy, and the conspirators decided that that would be a good time to carry out their plan. There was a snag almost immediately. The Baathist who was to block an intersection with his own car found that his car was blocked by a delivery van. Agreeing that they should postpone the assassination until another time, the gunmen suddenly saw Qassem's limousine approaching slowly on the narrow street. They decided to carry out the killing after all and quickly drew their automatic weapons.

## "The Plan Was Stupid"

Everything seemed to go wrong from that moment on. One member of the squad realized that he had forgotten to load his gun. Another had difficulty getting the gun's safety off, and could not shoot. Saddam, who was not supposed to be shooting at all, panicked and began firing at the slow-moving vehicle.

In the shooting, Qassem's driver was killed and one of his bodyguards was wounded. Qassem received only a superficial flesh wound and escaped by jumping into a taxi. One of the Baathist conspirators was killed by another bodyguard, and two others—including Saddam—were wounded in the crossfire.

Clearly the assassination attempt had been a disaster. "The plan was stupid," explains one man who was a Baathist at

# Saddam and the Leg Wound

*Saddam and the Baath Party have told and retold the story of his assassination attempt and the wound he received in the process. In Con Coughlin's book* Saddam: King of Terror, *the author shows how Saddam has benefited from making the injury far worse than it really was:*

Even though the injury Saddam sustained during the botched assassination attempt was negligible, the incident later became so embellished by Saddam's propaganda machine that most Iraqis were convinced that Saddam nearly died of his wounds. In an autobiographical film of Saddam's early life called *The Long Days*, which was made by Iraq's Ministry of Information in the 1980s, the wound was portrayed as being so serious that Saddam was unable to walk. In the film Saddam came across as a bold and heroic figure, who did not even flinch as a comrade used a pair of scissors to dig the bullet out of his leg. Saddam himself has continued to perpetuate this myth. When interviewed by an Egyptian journalist about the ordeal many years later, Saddam claimed he had been unhappy with the actor's depiction of him because it was unrealistic. "I wanted the director to reshoot the scene because I remember the day when it happened. I did not grimace or move an inch until the bullet was out."

that time. "The people who planned it weren't military men. They put the assassins on both sides of the street. Saddam was not injured by one of Qassem's guards. He was shot by one of his own comrades in the crossfire."[16]

## Many Versions of a Bullet Wound

There are several versions of Saddam's escape, although they all agree that he was wounded in the leg. According to Saddam, he managed to get to the safe house—the place where the squad agreed to meet afterward. He says that his leg was bleeding heavily by this time, but since he knew that if he went to a Baghdad hospital he would be recognized as one of the attackers, he organized and oversaw his own surgery.

In the "official" biography sanctioned by Saddam, the author wrote that Saddam, very seriously wounded, asked a fellow conspirator to dig the bullet from his leg. "Do you have the courage to do the operation, or do I have to do it myself?" Saddam asked, according to the biographer. When his coconspirator hesitated, Saddam ordered, "Bring me a new razor blade and a pair of scissors. Begin by cutting in the shape of a cross the flesh around the bullet; then sterilize the scissors, put it into the wound, and take out the slug. That's all."[17] However, that version differs from the one told by Dr. Muallah, who was called to the safe house to treat Saddam after the shooting. "When I went into the room I came across a pale, yellow young man," he recalls. "He told me he had a bullet wound, but when I treated him I found that he had nothing more than a grazed shin."[18]

Saddam and the others knew it was important that they leave Iraq for a time, for Qassem's police would be searching for them. Saddam went to Al-Ouja, possibly to say goodbye to his mother, and then crossed the border into Syria. After a few months, he slipped across the border into Egypt.

## In Exile

Saddam was safe as long as he was in exile, but he knew he was a wanted man in Iraq. To be caught by Qassem's men would be certain death for treason. In Damascus, Syria's capital, he met leaders of that country's Baathist Party, including Michel Aflaq, one of the founders of the movement. Aflaq was impressed with Saddam, and helped him become a full member of the Baath Party, rather than be merely hired muscle as he had been in Iraq.

Aflaq helped Saddam connect with a large group of young Baathists from Syria who were going to school in Cairo, Egypt. Egypt's President Nasser, who was still working for a worldwide brotherhood of Arabs, was no friend of Qassem's, and was pleased to meet one

of the men who had tried to assassinate him. With Nasser's help, Saddam, who had not even spent much time in high school back in Baghdad, enrolled in a Cairo high school and afterward, a small college.

At the start of his exile in Egypt in 1960, Saddam kept a low profile. One of President Nasser's associates recalls that the young man was almost an introvert:

> We helped him get into the [college] of law and tried to get him an apartment. . . . He used to come to see me now and then to talk about developments in Baghdad. He was quiet, disciplined, and didn't ask for extra funds like the other exiles. He didn't have much interest in alcohol and girls.[19]

After several months, however, Saddam began to have as much trouble with the law in Egypt as he had had in Iraq. He spent a great deal of time in cafés with his friends, often baiting other customers. One café owner remembers that Saddam would fight for any reason, often pulling out a pocketknife to threaten someone he did not like. The owner says that he tried to bar Saddam from coming to the café, but was told by police that the young man was under President Nasser's protection. Years later, he says that he was surprised that the same person became so famous. "I couldn't believe that such a bully who was picking fights all the time could grow up to be president of Iraq."[20]

# The Death of Qassem

*In their book* Saddam Hussein and the Crisis in the Gulf, *Judith Miller and Laurie Mylroie describe the uprising against Qassem, in which the Baath Party first gained power. Many Iraqi people were surprised and somewhat doubtful when they heard news of Qassem's death, so his murderers had to prove what had happened:*

Many people refused to believe that Qassem was dead. It was rumored that he had gone into hiding and would soon surface. The Baathists found a macabre way to demonstrate Qassem's mortality. They displayed his bullet-riddled body on television, night after night. As [witness] Samir al-Khalil ... tells it, "The body was propped upon a chair in the studio. A soldier sauntered around, handling its parts. The camera would cut to scenes of devastation at the Ministry of Defense where Qassem had made his last stand. There, on location, it lingered on the mutilated corpses of Qassem's entourage.... Back to the studio and close-ups now of the entry and exit points of each bullet hole. The whole macabre

sequence closes with a scene that must forever remain etched on the memory of all those who saw it: the soldier grabbed the lolling head by the hair, came right up close, and spat full face into it."

President Abdul Karim Qassem and two others lie murdered after the Baathist coup.

## The End of Qassem

It was during the time Saddam was in Egypt that the Baathists in Iraq were successful in assassinating President Qassem. Led by his uncle's old friend General Ahmad Hassan al-Bakr, the Baathists had help from a large group of army officers known as the National Guard. While the president's cadre of police and Communist supporters battled back, the Baathist conspirators executed Qassem and his closest aides in the palace.

When the news of the coup reached Saddam in Cairo, he was overjoyed. Not only had the Baathists—a party of only about one thousand members—achieved power, but he could return to Iraq and participate in the building of the new regime. He was even happier when he heard that the new prime minister was al-Bakr, who had first talked to him of the Baath Party.

Just when Saddam arrived in Baghdad is unclear; however, he did get there in time to participate in the street battles that raged for more than a month after Qassem's assassination. Not only were Communists fighting against the National Guard, but many of Iraq's poorest citizens who had liked Qassem's ideas on raising the nation's standard of living attacked the soldiers, too. Saddam, who had always enjoyed fighting in such situations, fought shoulder to shoulder with the National Guard, wearing their green armbands and wielding machine guns, killing anyone who dared defy the new government.

## "An Orgy of Violence"

Just what role Saddam would play in al-Bakr's new government was unclear at first. Soon after the coup, al-Bakr appointed a number of young Baathists to key positions in his new government, but Saddam was not among them. He had been gone for three years, and there were many who had risen in the ranks—far ahead of where Saddam had been previous to his exile. Saddam realized that he would have to wait and prove himself to the party leadership before he could play a significant role in the new regime.

As he tried to find a role among the Baathists, it was becoming very clear that the Baath Party could not expect to rule by popular demand. They had not won an election, nor had the public insisted that they replace Qassem. Quite the contrary, the Baath Party had seized the government by force, succeeding only because of the muscle of the National Guard. Each day since the February coup, there were violent attacks throughout the capital city by Communists and other groups protesting the new Baathist government.

If the Baathists were to remain in power, they would have to gain power over the rest of the army. They would have to eliminate as many political enemies as they could find. And finally, they would have to keep the Iraqi people frightened, so they would not think of plotting against the new government. To accomplish these ends, Saddam would prove to be a valuable part of the Baathist regime. His strength had always been his aggressiveness, and in the weeks and months following the coup, that would be exactly what al-Bakr and his government would need to survive.

## Chapter Three

# SADDAM THE KILLER

In March 1963, Prime Minister al-Bakr placed Saddam in charge of a special force that would identify and root out any Iraqis that could be possible enemies of the new government. The National Guard had already begun going from house to house in Baghdad, searching for people whose names were on a list of Communists and other enemies of the state. Those found by the National Guard were jailed until they could be interrogated by Saddam or one of his staff.

## Palace of the End

The headquarters for this interrogation force was called Palace of the End, so-called because it was where King Faisal and his family and staff were murdered in the coup of 1958. When the Baath Party took over, the palace was used as a setting for interrogation techniques that were unspeakably cruel.

Saddam's job was to question suspects about their activities, their families, and their associates. Suspects who would not talk were tortured—either until they could take no more and told him the information he sought, or until they died. Historians believe that it was at the Palace of the End that Saddam met Nadhim Kazzar, a notorious torturer, who taught Saddam a great deal about interrogation techniques. Kazzar was said to be so frightening in interrogation sessions, in fact, that even his fellow Baathists were afraid of him. One of his standard practices was to extinguish his cigarettes on the eyeballs of suspects.

As Saddam watched Kazzar, he learned a variety of ways to frighten and hurt his prisoners. One man who was tortured by Saddam in 1963 at the Palace of the End told of the pain he suffered:

> My arms and legs were tied together and I was hung by my feet from the ceiling. Saddam had converted a fan to take the weight of a man's body. As I was spun round, he beat me with a length of rubber hose filled with rubble.[21]

He felt lucky to have survived the torture, but hundreds of others were not as fortunate. After the interrogation squad had been operating for several months, one Iraqi described the grisly scene in the cellar of the Palace of the End. He said there were

> all sorts of loathsome instruments of torture, including electric wires with pincers, pointed iron stakes on which prisoners were made to sit, and a machine which still bore traces of chopped-off fingers. Small heaps of blooded clothing were scattered about, and there were pools [of blood] on the floor and stains all over the walls.[22]

Two men demonstrate electrical shock treatment, a torture technique used by the Iraqi secret police. Torture was a common interrogation method under Saddam.

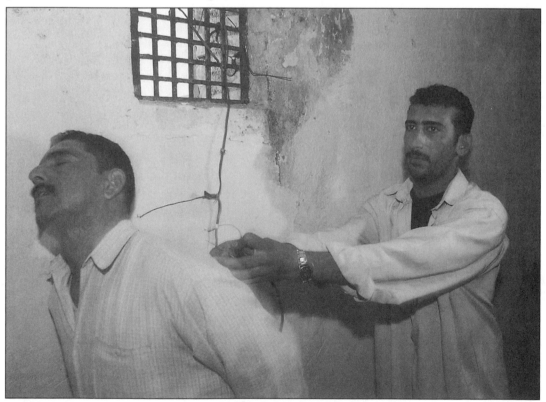

## A Split Party

While Saddam and his interrogation squad were busy, the Baath government was struggling to stay in power. They had not successfully attained control over the army, as they had hoped, and the National Guard (the paramilitary wing of the Baath Party) was too small to control all the uprisings throughout the country. Worst of all, infighting between various groups of Baathists made the party look tentative and weak.

It was not surprising when, in November 1963, just nine months after taking control of the government, the regular army—which was not aligned with the Baathist Party—marched on Baghdad and established a military dictatorship. Several of the most vocal Baath leaders were dismissed from duty by the military. Not all leaders could be easily dismissed, however, since the Baathists had been the majority party of the government since the previous election. Prime Minister al-Bakr, who had tried to be a voice of compromise and reason during this time, was allowed to remain as a less important part of the government, as were a few other Baathists.

## "Kill Them"

*Saddam was a strong believer that to solve any problem required a show of strength. In* The Outlaw State: Saddam Hussein's Quest for Power and the Gulf Crisis, *author Elaine Sciolino tells of two instances where Saddam instructed others how to use force to maintain power:*

Sahab al-Hakim, an Iraqi exile who lost 22 members of his family to Saddam's executioners, recalled an encounter that one of his friends ... once had with Saddam. "There was a time in the 1970s when the governor needed money for some projects in Najaf," said al-Hakim. "So he went to see Saddam. They sat on opposite ends of a long table. He asked for help. When he was finished, Saddam asked him, 'You need money?' He [the governor] answered, 'Yes, I need money.' So Saddam motioned to the bodyguard and asked for the bodyguard's gun. He shoved the gun to the other end of the table and said, 'Take it. And solve your problem yourself.'"...

Saddam even advised other heads of state to resolve their problems by force. [One Saudi official] recalled a conversation between Saddam and King Fahd, who was then crown prince, after Muslim fanatics seized the Grand Mosque in Mecca in 1979. Saddam ...had these words for the king: "Kill them. Kill everybody who went into the mosque. And kill everyone who identifies with them." King Fahd replied he hoped the matter could be resolved peacefully. But Saddam insisted, "No.... Don't waste your time. Kill all the male relatives, too. That way, there will be no one to take revenge."

Saddam wisely stayed as close to al-Bakr as possible, hoping to increase his own standing in the government. As a former general in the Iraqi army recalls:

Until 1963 Saddam Hussein was nothing more than a gangster. If you wanted someone killed, you called for Saddam. But after [al-]Bakr started to move up the party ranks to regain the status he had had before the military coup, Saddam was very smart and attached himself to him. [Al-]Bakr was a good politician, but he was useless in public. He was a backroom operator. He needed someone to carry out his orders, and so he asked Saddam. As a fellow Tikriti he believed Saddam was loyal to him, and so he gave Saddam a lot of responsibility. Saddam was therefore able to use [al-]Bakr to strengthen his position in the party.[23]

## "If There Is a Person, Then There Is a Problem"

Al-Bakr was elected to the top position in the Baath Party in 1964, and he chose Saddam as his deputy of security. Even though the Baathists did not have control of the government, al-Bakr and other members were secretly planning a takeover for some time in the future. Saddam would need to make sure that the party was strong on the inside before the takeover. That meant that any party members who were not supportive of al-Bakr

would need to be killed. A split within the party would spell disaster, as they had seen in November 1963. Saddam had studied the life of the Soviet dictator Joseph Stalin while in exile in Egypt, and Saddam agreed with Stalin who felt that killing political opponents was a necessary part of power. Saddam often repeated one of Stalin's rules: "If there is a person, then there is a problem; if there is no person, then there is no problem."[24]

Determined that there be no problems, Saddam established the *Jihaz Haneen*, or "Instrument of Yearning." This was the secret police force for the Baath Party. Not only was the *Haneen* politically aligned with the Baath Party, but it was comprised entirely of Tikritis. The strong tribal ties ensured that Saddam could trust the members of the *Haneen* completely. Accompanied by his burly squad of bodyguards, Saddam became even more notorious than ever before.

Rather than deny that he was a murderer, he sometimes flaunted it, say witnesses. He once walked into a Baghdad café to speak with some friends and loudly announced that he had just come from killing a man—a left-wing Baathist whose views were slightly different from those of al-Bakr. "I beat him over the head with my revolver," he said, "until he could move no more. You won't be seeing him again."[25]

Though Saddam's friends were loyal Baathists, they were horrified. They knew the man Saddam had attacked, and were sure he posed no threat to al-Bakr. One of the patrons said that they went to the hospital where the man had miraculously survived the beating. They tried to explain to the victim that they were appalled at Saddam's tactics. "We tried to impress upon him that we did not believe that this was what the party was all about," he says. "After what he had been through [fractured skull and two broken arms] it was difficult to make him understand that not everyone in the Baath Party was a homicidal maniac."[26]

## The Casual Coup

In 1967, al-Bakr began working out details of a new takeover. He knew, just as Saddam did, that anyone wishing to rule Iraq had to have power and force, for those things impressed people. Saddam was told to organize strikes and public demonstrations that showed the public's dissatisfaction with the military dictatorship, which was led by an ineffective president named Abdul Aref.

The demonstrations were violent and extremely effective. Some took place on the campus of Baghdad University, where students were already protesting President Aref's government. Though Saddam and the Baathists also disagreed with Aref's government, they wanted to prove their own personal power. They were anxious to show that they could have the upper hand—in reality, they were organizing these strikes as an opportunity to squelch them. "Saddam would arrive at the campus," recalls one witness,

firing his gun in the air to frighten the students and intimidate them.

He would run around with [his group of thugs] and force them back to class to resume their studies. The tactic worked brilliantly and the strike at the university was quickly broken.[27]

As the general public began to see evidence of the strength of the Baath Party, it seemed almost inevitable that there would be another government takeover. Surely with a party as strong and aggressive as the Baathists, the current government could not survive. When the takeover occurred on the morning of July 17, 1968, the coup was almost casual. Aref signed a letter of resignation, and the government switched hands. No blood was shed, no rioting occurred, for this time, not only the National Guard but also the majority of the army was supportive of the Baathists. Al-Bakr became the new president, and he appointed Saddam deputy secretary-general. Saddam was the second most powerful man in Iraq, and he was confident that he would rise even higher before too long.

## A Strong Start

The new government surprised many people at the beginning, for it accomplished some important improvements in Iraq. Using the motto We Came to Stay, al-Bakr and his colleagues continued to remind the Iraqi people that the Baathists were not simply one of a long string of government takeovers. They were firmly in control, and they intended to make Iraq a better place while they were in office.

Saddam Hussein poses as an American gangster to symbolize the strength and aggression of the Baath Party.

citizens and creating public housing for the poor.

In the first years of the Baathist regime, education was made a high priority. Iraq was very backward, with the majority of the people—especially the rural peasants—unable to read or write. Saddam, as deputy secretary-general, initiated a national reading project, including even the most remote desert villages. Reading classes were mandatory for every man, woman, and child, and anyone who did not attend could be jailed for three years.

Not surprisingly, few Iraqis risked skipping classes, for they were aware of the reputation of Saddam. The result was a rise in literacy—hundreds of thousands of Iraqis learned to read. Saddam was even honored by UNESCO, a branch of the United Nations, for his contribution to Iraq's literacy.

## "With One Word"

Many historians feel certain that Saddam wished to take over the presidency from al-Bakr immediately, but he held back, waiting until he himself had a solid base of support. Within days of the coup, Saddam moved to expand his secret police squad, which had primarily operated within Baghdad, to a nationwide

The Baathists spent millions of dollars on constructing roads, bridges, and hospitals. They also addressed the problem of poverty by breaking up some of the largest estates owned by the wealthy organization. He urged dozens of his fellow Tikritis, especially his cousins and other relatives, to attend the secret training schools of the *Jihaz Haneen* so they could join that organization.

Saddam also continued to display the force and violence for which he had become notorious. He vowed that this time, the Baathists would not lose power to another faction of the party, or to any other group within Iraq. That meant constant vigilance, keeping an eye on anyone who might criticize al-Bakr (or Saddam himself).

Anyone discovered or suspected to be an enemy of the regime was jailed and almost always killed within a very short time of his arrest. It was crucial, he believed, that people knew that the government would not tolerate dissent, and that it would be ruthless against its enemies. Saddam oversaw the interrogations himself, as one Iraqi journalist vividly remembers. "He was the man who gave the orders," he says. "He had the authority, with one word, to decide if you stayed alive or died."[28]

## Purges and Picnics

Saddam believed that the most effective means of exhibiting power was the purge, or widespread arresting of enemies. This attitude was another influence of his study of Joseph Stalin, who had been brutal to Russian people who he judged to be a threat to his power. Stalin had even targeted those he called "silent enemies"— people who did not commit any act of

treason, but had not turned in other people who had been guilty of treason. Saddam was impressed by the notion of silent enemies, and began targeting such people in Iraq. A single arrest might affect one's friends and immediate family, but a mass arrest of a dozen or more, Saddam believed, was an event everyone would notice.

The first Baathist purge was aimed at the Jews who lived in Iraq. A great deal of anti-Jewish sentiment existed throughout the Arab world. A purge of the Jews who lived in Baghdad would be a safe move politically, for Saddam knew that few Iraqis would protest. A few months after taking control of the country, the government announced that it had cracked a major Jewish spy ring in Iraq and had arrested sixteen spies who were sending important information back to Israel.

In truth, Saddam had personally arranged the entire operation. He had put the names of men he believed might be threats to him later on a list that he alleged was a spy network. In January 1969, the prisoners were put on trial before "judges" who were military officers without any legal training. Not surprisingly, the officers found the prisoners guilty. Hoping for a huge turnout at the public executions, which would be held in Baghdad at Liberation Square, the government proclaimed a national holiday. The Baathists even arranged for more than one hundred thousand people to be transported into Baghdad from other

A crowd in Baghdad views the bodies of two of the fourteen men hanged in 1969 on charges of spying for Israel.

cities and even from remote desert communities. In what was an almost carnival-like atmosphere, many families came with picnic lunches to watch the executions.

## "This Is Only the Beginning!"

People swarmed to Liberation Square, hoping to get a glimpse of the hangings while they ate their picnic lunches. Just before the men were killed, Saddam and President al-Bakr rode through the square in a white limousine, waving to the crowds. After the executions, President al-Bakr and other government leaders stood in front of the dangling bodies and made speeches about the danger of Jews and other enemies in Iraq. Though he had orchestrated the event, Saddam talked only briefly, telling the crowd that the men had been hanged that day to teach people a lesson. On the other hand, one

37

of al-Bakr's ministers, a very charismatic speaker, whipped the crowd into a frenzy with his angry words:

Great people of Iraq! The Iraq of today shall no more tolerate any traitor, spy, agent, or fifth columnist [subversive]! You foundling Israel, you imperialist Americans, and you Zionists, hear me! We will discover all your dirty tricks! We will punish your agents! We will hang all your spies, even if there are thousands of them! . . . Great Iraqi people! This is only the beginning! The great and immortal squares of Iraq will be filled up with the corpses of traitors and spies! Just wait![29]

## Seeing Danger Everywhere

The purge of the so-called espionage ring was only the first of many purges arranged by Saddam. Over the following months, he targeted a number of people besides Jews—Communists, fellow Baathists who aroused Saddam's suspicions, and the Shiite Muslims. The Shiites outnumbered the Sunnis in Iraq, and Saddam was worried that if they were to have a strong

## Saddam on Revolution

*In an interview with writer Fuad Matar in August 1979, Saddam explained his views on the importance of revolution in Iraq. The interview is contained in* The Saddam Hussein Reader, *edited by Turi Munthe.*

Revolution is a process that does not end with the application of its principles. It varies and changes shape according to the changing circumstances of life. That is why one's opinion of a revolution will develop as the revolution does and keep in step with the changes in the revolutionary leader and the revolutionary member of society. It is in the light of society's understanding of rights and duties that one can fully and correctly comprehend a revolution. That is why we find that the definition of democracy and liberty will change in shape and form as the revolution passes from one stage to another, depending on its success. The same applies to the revolution's stand against its enemies. Throughout its progress, a revolution must always remain in the service of the people for whom it essentially takes place. It is true that I always warn the revolutionary against the threats of . . . a new settled life that may make him a prey to illegal desires, making him forget his nationalist duties and obligations. However, this does not mean that I forget that the revolutionary is a human being entitled to his rights like any other ordinary human being, as long as those rights and needs are legal.

leader, they might overwhelm the ruling minority.

One Shiite leader in particular made Saddam nervous. He was Seyyed Mahdi al-Hakim, a much-loved religious figure. When he visited Baghdad, the streets were jammed with people stretching their arms to al-Hakim, hoping to receive his blessing. To murder al-Hakim would be too obvious, so Saddam bribed a jailed traitor, promising the man freedom if he would announce on television that al-Hakim's son was a spy. While not everyone believed the accusation, al-Hakim was so humiliated, he never returned to Baghdad—which decreased his base of support among the Iraqis there.

Many of the purges Saddam committed were based on trumped-up evidence, against people who had no plans to conspire against the government. However, in 1973, Saddam discovered a plot to kill both al-Bakr and himself. It was headed by his mentor in interrogation and torture, Nadhim Kazzar, who had been promoted to head of the internal security in the al-Bakr government, and had begun to expand his own power within the government. As Kazzar and forty-four coconspirators were arrested and executed, it was a betrayal that only fueled Saddam's belief that almost no one could be trusted.

## Eyeing the Presidency

Saddam was willing to be the number-two man in Iraq for a time, but with each passing month he was more and more impatient. He eyed the presidency, waiting for the right moment to assume control. With each arrest or murder of a political opponent, Saddam knew that he was securing his future power.

It was no secret that Saddam was the power behind President al-Bakr. Even though he occupied the number-two spot in the government, it was Saddam who was actually in charge. President al-Bakr had gradually become little more than a figurehead, giving speeches and making appearances at government functions. The real power was Saddam's because it was he who controlled the secret police. He was in charge of the networks of spies within the country and of those who gathered information. He controlled the interrogation squads, the torturers, and the National Guard, as well.

Although he had plans to take over the presidency, Saddam did not want to appear too eager—something that would offend al-Bakr's supporters. The president could be a congenial man, and crowds liked him. However, during his presidency, al-Bakr had suffered from poor health and a lack of stamina. More and more, he was willing to let Saddam make the decisions of the running of government.

Saddam was careful when asked about the relationship he had with the president. In one radio interview in Iraq, he denied that he was the more powerful of the two, and insisted that it was al-Bakr who was "the father and the leader."[30] However, many say that behind the scenes, he began putting pressure on al-Bakr to resign. One former Baathist recalls Saddam, together with his cousin Adnan, threatening al-Bakr in his office in July 1979: "They told him: 'You step down voluntarily and nothing will happen to you. But if we are forced to take action, it could be very unpleasant.'"[31]

## "The Leader"

In the weeks before he took over the presidency, Saddam knew it was important that he become more visible. While his job as interrogator and the head of secret police demanded that he work in the shadows, the Iraqi people now needed to see that Saddam was capable of being a national leader. He began appearing at news conferences and at public events.

He started visiting the neighborhoods in Baghdad to talk with people about how much the government had helped the common people. Saddam took advantage, too, of the journalists he kept on the payroll, ordering them to write articles that praised his leadership abilities. He insisted that he be referred to as "The Leader"—not as "Mr. Deputy," which he

Saddam Hussein attends an OPEC summit in place of Ahmad al-Bakr. Although al-Bakr was Iraq's president, Saddam was actually in charge of the country's affairs.

had been called before. To make certain that the people were reminded of him constantly, he ordered banners with his picture on them displayed in store windows and on walls throughout Iraq.

When al-Bakr announced on Iraqi radio on July 16, 1979, that he was stepping down as president, it was not a surprise to anyone. Al-Bakr gave no hint that he was being coerced; he assured the listeners that they would be governed well in the future. Saddam was, al-Bakr repeated, more than qualified to be their president.

## An Ominous Beginning

Saddam's first act as president was to summon hundreds of government and party officials to what he promised would be a special session of the new government. Because of Saddam's reputation, some of the officials were anxious; however, such a meeting did make sense. After all, with al-Bakr having stepped down, there was bound to be a bit of bureaucratic shifting.

The meeting was set for July 22, just six days after assuming the presidency. The large hall was crowded, and the officials talked quietly among themselves as they waited for the new president to speak. They were shocked when Saddam finally stood at the rostrum, for it looked as if he were holding back tears. Dabbing at his eyes with a large white handkerchief, he announced that he had been given bad news recently. Some government offi-

Saddam Hussein became Iraq's president in July 1979.

cials—some sitting there tonight—had betrayed him, he said.

There was a gasp from the audience as Saddam methodically began to list the names of the traitors. Witnesses later said that some of the men were so frightened as the names were read that they fainted. Many wept as they watched their friends and colleagues being ushered from the hall. One man whose name was read pleaded that he had done nothing at all wrong, but Saddam refused to listen. Saddam shouted, "*Itla! Itla!* [Get out! Get out!]"[32]

41

This was a purge, the first of Saddam's presidency. Those whom he targeted were men who had disagreed with him or who had been critical of his methods in the past. Saddam wanted to make certain that the new regime would have no critics from within the government. As the list of sixty men was read, Saddam asked those still seated what he should do with the traitors. Visibly relieved that they had been spared, the audience clapped and chanted their support for Saddam, and cried that a painless death was too good for a traitor.

The presidency of Saddam Hussein had officially begun.

## Chapter Four

# SADDAM THE PRESIDENT

Saddam had arranged to have the special session of the government on July 22 videotaped, and copies of the tape— including the bloody execution of the men afterward— sent to members of the Baath Party throughout Iraq. The tapes, which show Saddam calmly smoking a cigar as many of the accused are led screaming from the room, send a powerful message. The purge serves not only as a warning, notes one observer, "but also advertises to his subjects, his enemies, and his potential rivals that he is strong."[33]

## The Personality Cult

But while Saddam wanted Iraq's politicians to see the violent power of revenge, he was anxious for the Iraqi people to see a more benevolent power. He wanted people to see him as their friend, their hero, the champion of the nation. Early

in his presidency, he worked hard to create a sort of personality cult, a campaign to win the admiration and worship of the public. It was crucial, he told those closest to him, that "Saddam" and "Iraq" become synonymous in the minds of Iraqis.

Almost overnight, Baghdad and other Iraqi cities were awash in a blizzard of propaganda for the new president. He was pictured on T-shirts and caps, and on the face of most watches sold in Iraq. The airport in Baghdad was renamed Saddam International Airport, and every stamp and calendar bore his likeness. On every street corner was a large poster showing his smiling face.

Saddam insisted that all artistic production be placed under the control of the Baath Party, and therefore could be strictly censored. Poets and songwriters were urged to create verses that praised Saddam. These would be published and read at state functions and at festivals throughout the nation. "For those who conform," a human rights activist explained in 1981, "there are excellent rewards."[34] Saddam was reported to be especially pleased by the poetry that compared him to heroes or fierce animals. One poem often recited by Iraqi school children called Saddam "the perfume of Iraq, its dates, its estuary of the two rivers, its coast

and waters, its sword, its shield, the eagle whose grandeur dazzles the heavens. Since there was an Iraq, you were its awaited promised one."[35]

Within six months of Saddam's becoming president, there were at least two hundred other songs and poems written in praise of him. One was played every evening on television, after the news. Called "The Saddam Song," it was chanted over a background of fireworks and marching Iraqi soldiers:

During Saddam's reign, the Baath Party censored and controlled all forms of artistic expression.

# Turning the Clock Backward

*In her article "Tyranny of the Mind" for U.S. News & World Report, Marianne Szegedy-Maszak describes the way Saddam used fear to control the Iraqi people:*

When Iraqi-American psychotherapist Ilham al-Sarraf visited Iraq two years ago, she stayed in her 7-year-old nephew's room. In a place of honor at the head of his bed was a clock with a prominent picture of Saddam on its face. Unable to sleep with the dictator's image looming above her, Al-Sarraf turned the clock to the wall.

The next morning, when her nephew came in to gather his clothes, he asked her why "Baba Saddam"—Father Saddam—was facing the wall. Her brother and sister-in-law frantically tried to explain it away as a clumsy accident. What if the little boy told his teacher that his American aunt had acted disrespectfully toward Saddam Hussein? The landscape of Baghdad was haunted by the earless, the handless, the tongueless, the widowed and orphaned, who had endured capricious justice for lesser crimes. Seeing her brother "sweating bullets," Al-Sarraf quickly concocted an acceptable explanation. "It was no accident," she said. "I am a spiritual and religious woman, and I did not feel it was right to have a man looking at me while I slept in such skimpy clothes. That is why I turned the picture."

Oh Saddam, our victorious
Oh Saddam, our beloved;
You carry the nation's dawn
Between your eyes . . .
Oh Saddam, everything is good
With you . . .
Allah, Allah, we are happy;
Saddam lights our days [36]

## Omnipresent

Saddam also wanted the Iraqi people to identify with him, to see that he was very much like them. He and his wife now had five children, and he commissioned portraits of his family. He requested magazines photograph him at the beach, playing with his children, looking gentle and kind.

He began making public appearances throughout Iraq, too. Claiming that he wanted to hear the honest feelings of Iraqis about government and issues that were important to them, he visited even remote desert villages, as long as a television camera or a newspaper photographer was willing to tag along.

It began to seem that Saddam was everywhere, notes biographer Elaine Sciolino:

No aspect of Iraqi life was too insignificant for his attention. Whether it meant attending a ritual circumcision, lecturing to engineers on how to raise cattle, swinging a sickle with peasants in a wheat field, pulling on a fisherman's line, sitting cross-legged with Bedouins [nomadic desert people] sipping cardamon-laced coffee from thimble-sized cups, inspecting melons and radishes in a greengrocers' market—Saddam was there.[37]

## Worrying About Iran

Saddam said often that he planned on making Iraq the most powerful of the Middle East nations. However, there was a growing problem with Iran, Iraq's neighbor. In February 1979, only a few months before Saddam became president, there had been a change in the leadership of Iran. The shah, or king, was overthrown by a seventy-nine-year-old Shiite Muslim called the Ayatollah Khomeini.

A sworn enemy of the United States and its allies, the ayatollah also hated Saddam and the Sunni Muslims of Iraq. He wished to unite the Middle East not by any Arab brotherhood, as did Saddam, but by strict adherence to Islam. In fact, the ayatollah had announced that he wished to see the Shiites in Iraq rise up against Saddam. His speeches demonizing Saddam were more than words; he also exported money and weapons to Iraq Shiites, urging them to attack the new Iraqi government. "What we [he and his supporters] have done in Iran," stated the ayatollah, "we will do again in Iraq."[38]

It was soon clear that the ayatollah had great influence over the Shiites in

Iraq. On April 1, 1980, a militant Shiite lobbed a grenade at Tariq Aziz, Iraq's deputy prime minister. Although Aziz was not killed, the incident so alarmed Saddam that he began a massive campaign against Iraq's Shiite communities. Although they were the majority in Iraq, they did not have a strong leader to organize them. With the ayatollah in power across the border, however, they were a source of danger to Saddam's government.

## Terror Against the Shiites

Saddam unleashed his security forces on the Shiites, arresting thousands and hurling them into prisons and interrogation centers. One of the Shiite clerics, Muhammad Baqir al-Sadr, was tortured by having his beard set on fire. Afterward, Saddam's men drove nails through his head. Saddam wanted the methods of torture to get back to the Shiite communities so that people would be frightened.

Although the security forces killed clerics and other Muslim leaders, terrorist attacks on Iraqi government officials continued. As many as twenty officials were assassinated during the spring of 1980. The government widened its net, arresting any member of the Shiite communities—even those who were not actually suspected of wrongdoing. The Dawa Party, a political arm of the Shiites in Iraq, was a target, too. One man remembers Saddam's forces grabbing his month-old niece. "They put her on the table in front of her father," he says. "They began

# Watches

*In her book* The Outlaw State: Saddam Hussein's Quest for Power and the Gulf Crisis, *Elaine Sciolino compares the wristwatches made to celebrate Saddam's regime with those in Iran made to honor the ayatollah.*

There was one instance when the cult of Iran's Ayatollah Khomeini outdid the cult of Saddam. I call it "the cult of the watch." In the souks of Baghdad, there were watches with a portrait of a smiling Saddam on them. The photo of Saddam was muddy, the leather strap cheaply sewn, and the watch overpriced at more than $100 at the official exchange rate. Not so in Iran. The Swiss watch in honor of Khomeini that was sold at the beginning of Iran's revolution had a built-in light filter. Khomeini's stern face eerily appeared and disappeared twice a minute. Maybe it was supposed to be a sign that Khomeini was the "vanishing imam [holy

man]" who would someday, as the Shiites believe, bring heaven on earth. The watch was labeled Souvenir of the Islamic Republic. Its second hand was a red splotch—symbolizing a drop of martyr's blood. The watch cost $25 in Tehran's main bazaar. It still keeps perfect time.

Saddam watches like these were more expensive and less reliable than those made to honor Iran's ayatollah.

pulling her head, saying they would tear it off, and she was screaming."[39] The men finally released the baby, he says, after her father was told to stand and clap for Saddam, disavowing his ties to his Shiite faith. At least eighty-five thousand Shiites were executed or expelled from Iraq in 1980.

## A Declaration of War

On September 22, 1980, Saddam declared war on Iran. His goal was not only to overthrow the ayatollah's government, but also to reclaim the Shatt al-Arab, an important river at the head of the Persian Gulf, which was controlled at the time by Iran. He was confident that

Iraq would be victorious in two or three weeks' time, for Iran's army, because of the recent revolution, was hardly in a position to fight a major war.

At first it seemed as though his prediction would be accurate. As Iraqi forces swarmed across the border, they met lit-

Saddam Hussein launches a grenade during the Iran-Iraq War. Saddam waged war with Iran to overthrow Ayatollah Khomeini.

tle resistance. After several early victories, however, the Iraqi army stalled. They received little support from the Iraqi air force, for the nation was very large and Iraq had no air bases from which to launch strikes within Iran. There was simply too much space to control.

There was another important reason that Iraq's offensive stalled—Saddam himself. For years he had been filling the top positions in the army with men who were promoted because of their political loyalty to him rather than because of their military experience. This resulted in occasional battles lost because of poor decision making, and unwise use of military equipment.

Saddam was a hindrance to the generals of Iraq's army, too. He had always resented the fact that he had been turned down by the Baghdad Military Academy and that he had never had a military rank. In this war, however, he created the rank of field marshal for himself—which included a special uniform—and insisted on directing many of the battles personally. On the home front, the public saw videos of Field Marshal Saddam Hussein holding a rocket launcher, or bending over a map with his generals, discussing battle strategy. In truth, however, he added very little of value to Iraq's military.

Observers noted later that he frequently underestimated the enemy, while overestimating his own army's ability. Such lapses in judgment, notes biographer Con Coughlin, were often deadly for the Iraqi army. "Far from reducing [Iraqi] casualties," he writes, "Saddam's interventions, which were often diametrically opposed to the view of the professional soldiers, had devastating consequences."[40]

## An Unwise Decision

As the war went on, neither side was able to gain a decisive edge over the other. Saddam's boast of a speedy victory was not coming true. Even when the Iraqis managed to win a battle, hundreds or even thousands of their soldiers were killed in the process. By the end of October 1980, in fact, more than forty-five thousand Iraqis had been killed in Iran. A year later, with no end to the war in sight, the number of fatalities had reached one hundred thousand. Saddam called for a cease-fire in December 1981, but to his surprise, the ayatollah refused, and with renewed energy began striking at towns inside Iraq's borders.

The large death toll was having an effect on the army's morale. Soldiers who had been unclear about the reasons for the war in the first place felt a sense of hopelessness that they would ever return home. One intelligence report from a

Baghdad embassy in 1981 noted that "the Iraqis are suffering from no motivation, low morale, and extremely poor leadership. . . . The Iraqi army is not fighting for a cause but out of fear of persecution from Baath Party functionaries."[41]

In addition to the human toll, the expense of the war had become staggering. Iraq was spending $1 billion each month on weapons, ammunition, and supplies. At first, Iraq's plentiful oil reserves were paying for the war, but when Iran cut off Iraq's access to the Persian Gulf—the main route for Iraqi oil tankers—the oil industry all but collapsed. Iraq could produce oil, but unless it could deliver it to buyers, the product was useless to the economy. As a result, construction projects in Iraq, such as hospitals, roads, and schools, now stood incomplete. Unemployment rose, and people could no longer afford to purchase most of the imported goods they were used to buying.

## An Angry Public

While the standard of living in Iraq remained unchanged in the early months of the war, most people had been willing to support the Baath regime. However, as the war dragged on, the Iraqi people became discouraged. Almost every family in the country had lost a brother, a son, or a father in the war. Day after day, flag-draped coffins were being driven home from the front, either in truck beds or strapped to the tops of Iraqi taxis. Iraqi teenagers, many of whom had been

An Iraqi man mourns his father at a monument to honor more than one hundred thousand Iraqis who were killed during the Iran-Iraq War.

drafted for the duration of the war, were bitter. Many had delayed starting jobs, college, and getting married because of the war, and it seemed to be endless.

The blame fell on Saddam, for it was he who began the war. Realizing he was at risk from an angry public, Saddam stepped up the nation's security force. He used the new Republican Guard, the elite military squad that he controlled personally, which had replaced the Baath Party's National Guard. However, despite increased security from the Republican Guard to protect himself and his family, there were several attempts on his life. In July 1982, Saddam's motorcade was attacked by men with machine guns in the rural village of Dujail. The gunmen missed, however, and in retaliation for the assassination attempt, Saddam ordered the village destroyed by helicopters dropping napalm, a chemical that causes blindness and severe burns. Every house in Dujail was burned to the ground, and bulldozers came in two hours later and turned the area into a field, leaving no evidence that it had ever been inhabited.

Another attempt was made in his own hometown, Tikrit, when a car packed full of explosives was left on his motorcade route. Again, Saddam was saved because the fuses malfunctioned, detonating the explosives an hour before he arrived in town.

## Fighting Back

Saddam knew that he had to answer such attempts with toughness. He began spending more time in Baghdad, and less time at the front "helping" the army. One of the first things on his agenda was a meeting with the National Assembly, the legislative arm of the government. He was aware that some of the assemblymen had had reservations about his attack on Iran in the first place and recently had become outspoken in their opposition to the war.

When Saddam heard that one of his cabinet ministers had suggested that he step down and let former president al-Bakr negotiate a peace with Iran, Saddam suggested that the two of them go into an adjoining room to discuss the matter more fully. A moment later, say witnesses, "A shot was heard and Saddam returned alone to the cabinet as though nothing had happened. . . . When the dead man's wife asked for the return of her husband's body, it was delivered to her chopped into pieces."[42]

Several meetings ended with Saddam murdering someone. During one meeting, he noticed that two men were passing a note back and forth. Correctly assuming that they were communicating about overthrowing him, Saddam drew his gun without a word and shot them both. He was no less direct in dealing with critics in the military. In the summer of 1982, when Iran was making fierce attacks on Iraq, there were many officers who were critical of the war policy. In response, Saddam ordered that at least three hundred high-ranking officers be executed.

## An Upbeat Image

While he was executing critics at the front and behind closed doors of government, Saddam believed that it was important to keep a positive public image. He wanted to appear confident in the army, even though he was privately very worried. He knew that if the Iraqi people sensed that he was anxious or unsure, they would rise up against him.

He ordered more portraits of himself displayed throughout Baghdad and other cities, knowing that it was crucial for him to be a visible presence everywhere in Iraq. Even before the war, there had been posters on almost every street corner. But now one could not walk for two minutes without seeing at least one twenty-foot-tall poster. Some of the posters showed him in army fatigues. In others he was portrayed as an ancient war hero, riding a white stallion and brandishing a sword. Although Iraqis would not dare make fun of the number of posters of their president, many visitors to Iraq did. One popular joke at the time was that the nation's population had recently soared to 26 million—13 million Iraqis and 13 million pictures of Saddam.

Besides a powerful, heroic image, Saddam wanted to show a sympathetic side, too. One way he accomplished this was by creating a policy of rewarding grieving families who had lost a family member in the war. Fathers who had lost sons in battle were given a Rolex watch, complete with Saddam's picture on the face of the watch. The family was presented with a new car, a plot of land, and a low-interest loan so that they could purchase a home if they did not already own one. He also created dozens of new medals so that every widow would have a colorful remembrance of her husband's sacrifice for Iraq.

To appear confident and strong to the Iraqi army and people, Saddam Hussein ordered portraits like this one to be displayed in cities throughout Iraq.

While his generosity toward the Iraqi people was highly publicized, Saddam insisted that the public could not learn how many soldiers were dying. If they knew that the number of deaths in some battles reached more than five thousand, for example, there would almost surely be rioting in the streets. Instead, the government began falsifying news of the war. When hundreds or even thousands of Iraqis were killed in battle, some of the bodies were kept in freezers and released weeks or even months later. When a family did receive their loved one's remains, they were forced to comply with a new law that banned public funerals.

## An Empty War Chest

As the war dragged on, Saddam worried about Iraq's dwindling resources. The army could not afford to replace the tanks and planes that were lost, and Saddam was forced to ask for help from other Middle Eastern nations. Kuwait, Jordan, and Turkey were willing to allow Saddam to build pipelines and transport routes for Iraq's oil through their countries, since Iran had seized control of the Persian Gulf. That helped, for without the revenue from oil sales, Iraq was losing more than $30 million each day.

In addition to creating ways to sell Iraq's oil, Saddam appealed to the Iraqi people for help. He appeared on television, beginning in 1983, asking for people to help the war effort by donating gold, jewelry, or cash. Although he at first phrased his appeals as though he were asking for help, it was soon clear that the donations were mandatory. Soldiers were sent door-to-door, asking people for their possessions that could be sold.

At the same time Saddam was seen each evening on television, greeting some of those who had given large amounts, he also appeared to be making veiled threats to the viewing audience who did not choose to contribute, or who did not give enough. In one appearance, he told the story of a millionaire from his hometown of Tikrit, who had sent only three thousand dollars and a dagger. "How much faith does this man have in his homeland and in the revolution?" he thundered, furious that the man with so much money should give so little. He smiled and then added ominously, "I'm sure he will hear me."[43]

## "More Deadly than Taking Poison"

The ayatollah had suffered as much backlash for the war in Iran as Saddam had in Iraq. Even so, Iran refused the United Nations' request for a settlement and mounted a strong invasion against some of Iraq's bigger cities. The Iraqis fought back—perhaps with more spirit, since they were now defending their homeland, say historians—and the attack was repelled. The United States, nervous that the situation in the Middle East would spread and interfere with oil production, sent warships to patrol the Persian Gulf to make certain that Iran did not interfere with Kuwait's oil tankers.

As the war stalled in 1988, Iran finally agreed to the United Nations' plan for a cease-fire, and Saddam was jubilant. The ayatollah, on the other hand, was frustrated, for he had wanted Muslims throughout the Middle East to rise up against Saddam. "I had promised to fight to the last drop of my blood and to my last breath," he announced on a Tehran radio station. "Taking this decision was more deadly than taking poison. I submitted myself to God's will and drank this drink for His satisfaction."[44]

Saddam ignored the ayatollah's bitter words and declared himself the victor of the long war. Eight years after it began, Saddam's war was finally over.

## Chapter Five

# A New Path to War

Not surprisingly, the Iraqi people were ecstatic when the war finally ended. For weeks, there were celebrations throughout the nation, as people danced, sang, and cheered. They had been living in a state of war for eight years and felt as if it was time now to enjoy a life of peace.

But Saddam was aware that their joy would be short lived. As he watched hundreds of thousands of Baghdad residents celebrating the war's end, say witnesses, Saddam was already envisioning the dark days ahead, when the people would rise up against him. The main reason they would rebel, he knew, would be the poor economy.

## Twelve Dollar Shampoo

Iraq had not only used up most of its own finances during the war, but had borrowed heavily from other nations. "Saddam had fought the war on credit," notes one biographer.

By the end of the war, he owed $25.7 billion to Saudi Arabia, $10 billion to Kuwait, and smaller sums to other Arab states. An additional $40 billion was owed to the United States [not for weapons, but for a loan of cash], Europe, and the rest of the industrialized world.[45]

Saddam knew that the chances of repaying these loans were almost nil. His economy was in ruins; there were few jobs, especially for the 1 million soldiers returning home after the long war. As a result of the massive unemployment, people had less money to buy, and Iraqi factories scaled production back—which created a short supply of Iraqi-made goods. On the other hand, imported goods were abundant but ridiculously expensive—a bottle of shampoo from Jordan cost twelve dollars, while a single roll of film was twenty-one dollars. Some financial experts estimated that it would take an infusion of $230 billion just to stabilize the economy.

Because of these economic problems, Saddam knew he could not repay the debts. He sent diplomats to Kuwait and Saudi Arabia to demand that those countries' leaders not only forgive those outstanding loans, but grant new ones. After being turned down, Saddam made vague threats to those nations, warning them of dire consequences if they did not issue him the loans. Unconcerned about such threats, neither nation wrote off the loans, nor was any more money lent to Iraq.

## Saying "No" to Freedom

Another reason Saddam had reason to worry about the people's support was that their expectations of more freedom in Iraq were not being met. Iraqis had hoped that after the war there would be a relaxing of the rigid police state in which they had been living. During wartime, Iraqis had not been permitted to travel or to read foreign newspapers. Saddam had hinted during the war that he might be open to more freedoms after it was over.

However, in the months after the war, he was uneasy about loosening the controls he had created. He agreed to allow some international travel, but he did not want to allow people to vote on members

of the National Assembly. Saddam and his security forces had worked hard at eliminating many of his political enemies and the thought of allowing new members in was frightening. As his popularity with the public continued to sink, however, he compromised. He would allow people to vote in elections, but he reserved the right to have the final word on what candidates could run.

## A Worsening Image

Saddam's family was another reason his image was worsening. When his children were small, Saddam had encouraged publicity photographs of his family. His children were now grown, however, and their activities—especially those of his two sons—had created a great deal of negative attention for Saddam, and definitely added more problems to his struggling presidential image. This negative publicity was another reason that Saddam was willing to compromise on certain issues with the Iraqi people.

There was no doubt that Uday, Saddam's oldest, was the worst. He had been a bully as a teenager, but now that he was a young man, his violent tendencies and heavy drinking made him dangerous. One of the few young Iraqi men not serving in the army during the Iran-Iraq War, Uday spent his time going from bar to bar in Baghdad, starting fights and picking up young women. Uday had once been viewed as Saddam's political heir, but recent events had brought shame and embarrassment to the family.

# Iraq's New War Monument

*In their book* Out of the Ashes: The Resurrection of Saddam Hussein, *Andrew Cockburn and Patrick Cockburn describe the monument unveiled after the Iran-Iraq War to honor Iraq's dead:*

The victory of Iraq was real, but Saddam grossly exaggerated its extent. This was under-lined on August 8, 1988, a year after the end of the fighting, when an extraordinary mon-ument was opened in Baghdad. It was an Iraqi Arc de Triomphe. Two metal forearms, each forty feet long, reach out of the ground clutching steel sabers, whose tips cross, forming an arch under which the Iraqi army passed. The arms were modeled from a cast taken of Saddam's own arms. They were too big to be made in Iraq and were cast in a metal foundry in Basingstoke, England. The invitation to guests for the inauguration of the monument captures the flavor of the event:

"The ground bursts open and from it springs the arm that represents power and deter-mination, carrying the sword of Qadissiya [the location of an ancient battle in which the Arab army defeated the Persians]. It is the arm of the Leader President Saddam Hussein (God preserve and watch over him) enlarged forty times. It springs out to announce the good news of victory to all Iraqis and pulls in its wake a net that has been filled with the helmets of the enemy."

**Saddam Hussein's monument to honor the Iraqis who died during the Iran-Iraq War stands tall over a Baghdad street.**

Saddam Hussein's oldest son Uday (right) was accused of murder in the late 1980s. The dictator initially denounced his son, ordering that he be arrested and tried for the crime.

Uday had learned that Kamel Hanna Jajjo, his father's food taster and bodyguard, had introduced Saddam to a woman, who would eventually become his wife. The law allowed multiple marriages, but Uday felt that his father's taking a second wife was a betrayal to Sajida, Uday's mother. Furious that it had been Jajjo who introduced the two, Uday went to a party that he knew Jajjo would attend. In front of guests, he walked up to the bodyguard and killed him with a club. Witnesses say that Uday continued to beat the man long after he was dead.

## "Your Man Is Going to Kill Me"

Saddam, who had often intervened when his children ran afoul of the law, was furious this time. He denounced Uday on Iraqi television, and ordered that he be arrested and charged with murder. According to one Iraqi account, a distraught Uday took a bottle of sleeping pills and was rushed to the hospital. "As they were pumping out his stomach,

Saddam arrived in the emergency room, pushed the doctors aside, and hit him in the face, shouting: 'Your blood will flow like my friend's.'"[46]

Uday was arrested, and Saddam was unmoved by Sajida's pleas for her son's release. After Uday attacked a prison guard and was consequently beaten, he wrote to Sajida. "Your man [Saddam] is going to kill me." He demanded that she find someone who could "release me from this torture. I will either die or I will go crazy."[47]

Eventually Saddam did relent and released Uday from prison if his son promised to stay in Switzerland for a time. Uday agreed; however, his exile ended prematurely when he was arrested for attacking a Geneva police officer with a knife and was sent back to Baghdad. With sto-ries such as these circulating in Iraq, it is not surprising that Saddam's image was worsening among the Iraqi people.

## An Unspeakable Atrocity

It was not only in Iraq, however, that Saddam's reputation was eroding. News of his dealings during the war with the Kurds, a non-Arab people in northern Iraq, was circulating, and the stories were appalling. Saddam had put his cousin, General Ali Hassan al-Majid, in charge of a campaign to subjugate the Kurds, who Saddam believed were fighting with the Iranian troops against Iraq. The general was often known as "Chemical Ali" because he preferred using nonconventional weapons such as gas and other poisons when possible.

# Uday

*Saddam's oldest son, Uday, was notorious throughout Iraq because of his short temper and insatiable appetite for cruelty, as Con Coughlin explains in this excerpt from* Saddam: King of Terror.

Despite his incredible wealth, Uday harbored a sadistic streak from which not even his closest colleagues and advisers were immune. On one occasion, Abbas Janabi [Uday's private secretary] inadvertently upset Uday by writing an article about the state of the Iraqi army. He was jailed and tortured. [Janabi recounts:] "Uday sent one of his bodyguards to the prison and he used a pair of pliers to pull out one of my teeth. Then he wrapped it in a Kleenex and took it to Uday to show he had done the job." On another occasion, Janabi saw Uday torture a man who had looked after his business interests in Jordan, beating him with a baseball bat on the soles of his feet, then suspending him from a revolving ceiling fan and flogging him with a cable. During the fifteen years he worked for Uday, Janabi was jailed on eleven separate occasions.

This Kurdish boy was burned by Iraqi troops during a chemical weapons attack. In May 1987, Saddam Hussein ordered that chemical weapons be used against the Kurds.

With Saddam's approval, more than ten thousand Kurds had been executed and buried in mass graves in northern Iraq. He had also deported Kurds from more than twelve hundred villages and towns, relocating them in concentration camps and then razing each of the villages. When the Kurdish population tried to resist, General al-Majid began using his chemical weapons. The first chemical attacks occurred in May 1987, but the most horrendous attacks occured just a few months before the war ended, in March 1988, in the city of seventy thousand called Halabja, not far from the Iran border in northeast Iraq.

## Pink, White, and Yellow Clouds

Nasreen, a young Kurdish woman, was sixteen when Halabja was attacked. She saw an Iraqi helicopter flying low over the town, the men on board taking pictures with a video camera. The bombardment occurred less than an hour later. She was preparing food for her family when she heard the planes flying over. Instead of explosions, however, Nasreen heard the sound of metal canisters hitting the ground. There were pink, white, and yellow clouds rising from the canisters, each releasing an odd smell, she recalls. "At first it smelled bad," she says, "like garbage. And then it was a good smell, like sweet apples. Then like eggs."[48]

As she looked outside, she could see that the family's animals were being affected by the clouds:

It was very quiet, but the animals were dying. I told everybody that there was something wrong. There was something wrong with the air. . . . Our cow was lying on its side. It was breathing very heavily, as if it had been running. The leaves were falling off the trees, even though it was spring. . . . There were smoke clouds around, clinging to the ground. The gas was heavier than the air, and it was finding the wells and going down the wells.[49]

Throughout the town, people were frightened, but no one was sure what to do. Some sought refuge in cellars, hoping the gas would not reach them. "We wanted to stay in hiding, even though we were getting sick," says one woman, who felt a sharp pain like stinging needles in her eyes from the gas. "My sister came close to my face and said, 'Your eyes are very red.' Then the children started throwing up. They kept throwing up. They were in so much pain, and crying so much."[50]

## "The Lesser of Two Evils"

In the end, more than five thousand residents of Halabja died from the attacks of what proved to be a combination of nerve gas and mustard gas. Twice that many suffered skin-shredding burns, convulsions, scorched lungs, and bleeding kidneys. Many who survived would be plagued with cancer, abnormally high rates of miscarriage, blindness, and birth defects among their children. The attacks halted the Kurdish rebellion.

One Kurdish leader noted, "We cannot fight chemical weapons with our bare hands."[51]

As newspapers around the world began documenting the use of the illegal gas against the Kurds, there was some embarrassment on the part of some nations. During the Iran-Iraq War, the United States and several nations of Western Europe had given assistance to Iraq, even though they had reasons to be wary of Saddam. They felt that the extremist revolutionary politics of the ayatollah in Iran could spread to the rest of the Middle East and destabilize the region. For nations that depended so highly on the Middle East's oil, this would be trouble. "There was a huge consensus," says one U.S. government official, "that Saddam was the lesser of two evils."[52] Geoffrey Kemp, a key member of the National Security Council, put it more plainly: "It wasn't that we wanted Iraq to win the war, we did not want Iraq to lose. We really weren't naive. We knew he was an SOB, but he was our SOB."[53]

It was Germany, in fact, that had helped Iraq develop a chemical plant to create the hydrogen cyanide compound. That said, the use of the weapons on Kurdish men, women, children, and babies was appalling, and throughout the world Saddam was condemned for his actions. Not only was the use of such weapons banned by the Geneva Convention's rules of warfare, but Saddam had become the only leader in history besides Adolf Hitler who had used such poisons on his own people.

## Going on Offense

With his family situation fodder for tabloids and his international reputation in tatters, Saddam knew that his control of Iraq was in peril. What he needed most was an infusion of money to stabilize Iraq's economy and to divert the negative attention from himself. In 1989, he began to stir up trouble with Kuwait. Saddam had already asked for his wartime loans to be forgiven and had been turned down.

This time, he did not ask—he demanded. He claimed that two islands which Kuwait owned, Warba and Bubiyan, should by all rights be Iraq's. He ordered Kuwait to turn over the islands so that Iraq's oil industry could construct a shipping port on the site. He also accused Kuwait of stealing oil from an Iraqi oil field next to the Kuwait border, and demanded that the borders be redrawn between the two countries. If he had access to the rich oil fields of Kuwait, it would greatly help his economy. Further, he lashed out at the Kuwaitis who were producing more oil than necessary, and thereby driving the price per barrel lower—which hurt Iraq. "We have warned them," Saddam stated to the Iraqi people. "It is a conspiracy to make us live in famine."[54]

He then turned his attention to the United States, which had kept a presence in the Persian Gulf supporting Iraq since the war. Now Saddam demanded that the U.S. ships leave the Gulf, and requested that the nations of the West leave the

Middle East. He threatened to retaliate against the United States if it became involved in the dispute between Iraq and Kuwait. "If you use pressure," he warned, "we will deploy pressure and force. We cannot come all the way to you in the United States, but individual Arabs may reach you."[55]

## "The 19th Province of Iraq"

Even though Saddam's words were combative, few believed that war was imminent. However, on July 21, 1990, Saddam gave the order for thirty thousand Iraqi troops to assemble at Kuwait's border. Kuwait had already slowed their production of oil, creating a rise in prices,

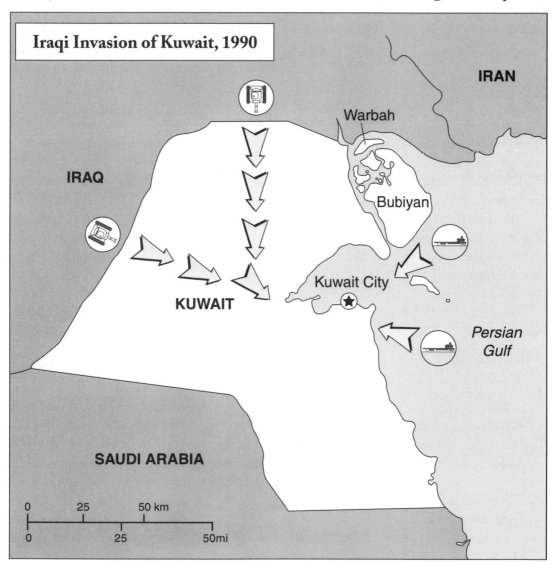

Iraqi Invasion of Kuwait, 1990

but Saddam still threatened. He moved more troops to the border—one hundred thousand in all, plus three hundred tanks—but still no one in the Arab world or the West believed Saddam would start another war.

At 2:00 A.M. on August 2, 1990, Saddam's troops rolled across the border into Kuwait. The Kuwaiti army, which was woefully outnumbered, barely resisted, and the invasion was over in less than seven hours. Chemical Ali was given the job of rounding up Kuwaiti men for questioning, detainment, and later, execution. Barbara Bodine, a key American diplomat in Kuwait, vividly remembers the brutality of the Iraqi treatment of the Kuwaitis. "The husband of a friend of mine was a police officer," she says. "He was taken away by the Iraqis. The next day, the doorbell rang. His wife saw on her doorstep what she presumed to be the fingernails and eyeballs of her husband."[56]

Meanwhile, the Iraqi soldiers, who had arrived by the busload, looted and burned most of Kuwait's public buildings. "The finest art of the Islamic Empire, painstakingly collected with Kuwait's copious oil revenues, was trucked to Baghdad," one reporter noted. "Private homes gave up their fine carpets, and stores surrendered their inventories."[57]

The Baath Party celebrated in Baghdad, calling Kuwait "the 19th province of Iraq," and stating confidently that "the Kuwaiti branch has returned to the Iraqi tree."[58] Saddam believed that there would be no intervention by other nations, although he would learn otherwise very soon.

## Resolutions and a Military Response

Within a few days of Saddam's occupation of Kuwait, the United Nations passed a resolution that demanded that Iraq leave Kuwait by January 15, 1991. Further, the United States and a group of other nations imposed trade sanctions on Iraq. Not only would they stop buying Iraq's oil, but they would stop exporting the products Iraq purchased from them on a regular basis.

In addition, they made certain that Saddam could not simply buy such products from other nations. Because much of Iraq's money was in banks throughout Western Europe and even the United States, those accounts were frozen until Saddam agreed to leave Kuwait. As the weeks passed, however, there was no sign that Saddam would leave.

In the fall of 1990, the United Nations passed another resolution, ordering Saddam to leave Kuwait by January 15, 1991. If Saddam failed to meet that deadline, he would face attack from a UN coalition, an army made up of soldiers from thirty nations. Still Saddam did not respond, and as a result, U.S. ships began to prowl the waters of the Persian Gulf so that Iraqi oil tankers would not be able to leave.

# Call for Jihad

*In September 1990, Saddam Hussein issued a call for jihad, or holy war, against the United States prior to Desert Storm. In this excerpt from the speech, which is contained in* The Saddam Hussein Reader, *edited by Turi Munthe, Saddam assures the Iraqi people that they will surely be victorious.*

As for America's sea and air fleets, its armies and those who slipped with it into the abyss, they will only strengthen in us, the leadership, and the great people of Iraq, our faith in the path that we have chosen in order that God, the people, the nation, and humanity may bless us. The rattling of their weapons and the use of these weapons will only increase our determination to respond to sincere principles, their slogans and their applications, in social justice, in rejecting tyranny, division, and weakness. The motto of the faithful is: There is no going back; the believer will advance. This is our eternal motto which will not be dropped from our hands. Under the banner of faith and jihad, many heads will roll— heads that have never been filled with pride and whose owners never knew the path of faith. Let those who have been promised martyrdom have it. . . .

Have you known, O brothers, in the history you have studied of someone who tried to starve a nation to death by preventing food from reaching them? Have you seen the acts of Nazism, which the West rants on about, claiming to hoist the banner of confrontation and comparing it to everything loathsome and inhuman, . . . cut off medicine from a whole nation so the sick will die because there is no medicine? . . . The Arab and Iraqi nation will not forget their evil deed.

## "Don't Be Afraid"

While the Iraqi forces had celebrated their easy victory over Kuwait, they began to worry as the UN deadline loomed closer. Saddam had been confident that there would be no interference in a war between two Arab nations, but clearly he was wrong. And as UN troops began to mass at the border, the Iraqi soldiers were frightened. They had outnumbered Kuwait's army, but they could not hope to outgun the army of the coalition.

The fears of the soldiers were felt by Saddam's military advisers, too. One former Iraqi general remembers meeting with Saddam just two days before the UN coalition was due to attack. "[Saddam] told us, 'Don't be afraid. I see the gates of Jerusalem open before me,'" the man recalls. "I thought, '*What is this . . .* ?' Baghdad was about to be hit with this terrible firestorm, and he's talking to us about visions of liberating Palestine?"[59]

Wafic Samurrai, Saddam's chief of intelligence, was equally bewildered. He had worked for Saddam long enough to know that it was suicide to disagree with him, but in this situation, he had no choice. He explained to Saddam that there was no possible way they could win this war. Saddam refused to listen, maintaining that he had a foolproof plan. Iraqi troops would capture U.S. soldiers and tie them up around Iraqi tanks and arsenals. The Americans would be human shields, and the coalition army would not dare fire on such targets, for fear of killing their own men.

Although Saddam clearly believed his plan had merit, Samurrai, according to one report,

Saddam Hussein's army easily overpowered Kuwait in 1990 but was outnumbered by the U.S.-led coalition the next year.

knew that this was nothing more than a hallucination. How were the Iraqis supposed to capture thousands of American soldiers? . . . Even if it could be done, the very idea of using soldiers as human shields was repulsive, against all laws and international agreements. Who knew how the Americans would respond to such an act?[60]

## "How Sweet Victory Is"

Last-minute negotiations offered by the United Nations were rejected by Saddam, who threatened to use weapons of mass destruction—nuclear, chemical, and biological warheads—which could be attached to missiles. Most experts did not believe he had developed nuclear weapons, but no one doubted that he possessed both biological and chemical weapons.

As if taunting the coalition forces, Saddam predicted an easy victory for Iraq. It would be, he promised the Iraqi people, "the great duel, the mother of all battles, between the great right [Iraq] and the evil that will certainly be defeated."[61] He warned the Kurds in Iraq that they should not even consider helping any coalition forces that tried to invade Iraq. "If you have forgotten Halabja," he said, "I would like to remind you that we are ready to repeat the operation."[62] Few doubted that he was serious.

His boasts were groundless, however. Two days after Iraq's deadline, the UN forces attacked in a war known as Desert Storm, and it was over quickly. After mounting intensive air strikes, UN ground troops entered Kuwait and Iraq. The Iraqi army never had a chance; more than 150,000 were killed, fifty thousand were taken prisoner, and a great number of them ran away, abandoning tanks and large artillery guns. The coalition declared victory on February 27, 1991, though Saddam saw it otherwise. On Iraqi television, Saddam praised the Iraqis for having the courage to fight—a fact which made them the true victors. "You have faced the whole world, great Iraqis," he announced on Iraqi television. "You have won. You are victorious. How sweet victory is."[63]

# Chapter Six

# Saddam
# Surviving

It was clear immediately after Desert Storm that Saddam's invasion of Kuwait had resulted in an extensive amount of damage to Iraq—and to Saddam's image, as well. Baghdad, writes reporter Sandra Mackey, "was a city with its bones broken and its tendons cut."[64] There was no electricity, no running water, and each day millions of gallons of untreated sewage flowed into the Tigris River, causing widespread disease among the 4 million people who lived there. Many of the city's most important buildings were burned-out shells, traffic lights and telephones did not work, and medical care was nonexistent because of a lack of medicine and equipment. Mounds of garbage and human waste were found on every street.

## "Down, Down with Saddam"

But it was more than the physical reminders of the war that caused Saddam problems. It was the fact that throughout the country, people were rebelling in ways they had never done before. Deserters from the army came home cursing the president who had promised them victory, yet had let them linger in Kuwait only to be bombarded by the coalition force. "Some soldiers," notes one reporter, "spoke openly of their hatred of the leader who, even in defeat, insisted they had won the war."[65]

Armed rebels in cities and towns throughout Iraq battled what was left of Saddam's army and police. Shiites revolted, and Kurds took back territory that had been seized from them by Saddam's soldiers. By March 1991, Saddam had lost control of fourteen of Iraq's eighteen provinces. For the first time since he became president, Saddam's posters and statues were defaced. In Basra, a large city in southern Iraq, opponents of Saddam and his Baath Party scrawled "Down, Down with Saddam" on the sides of buildings.

Many world leaders, including President George H. Bush of the United States, hoped that Saddam would be replaced by his angry citizens. Even while the war had still been going on, Bush had called for revolt, calling on "the Iraqi military and the Iraqi people to take matters into their own hands and force Saddam Hussein, the dictator, to step aside."[66]

## Fighting Back

If people thought that Saddam would simply give up, they were mistaken. He had no intention of allowing anyone to take over his position in government. In March, soon after the cease-fire, Saddam appealed to the Iraqi people by reminding them how poor Iraq had been before the Baathists took office. He told them that the nation could never rebuild as long as people were battling one another. "Is it democracy and patriotism," he asked, "to break Iraq up into sects and ethnic

Iraqi children rummage through garbage in search of food. The Gulf War devastated the infrastructure of Iraq, creating severe shortages of food and medicine.

communities fighting among themselves?"[67]

But the most persuasive aspect of his power had not been his diplomacy, but rather his cruel displays of power. To reclaim the degree of power he had held previously, he needed to reestablish the loyalty of his army. He set about reorganizing the bureaucracy of the army, building a strong central command from those Tikritis he was sure he could trust. Any other officer who had doubted his leadership or criticized his methods was arrested and executed. Once he felt as though he had control of the army, he doubled their pay and gave them an assignment that was sure to be successful—putting down the Shiite and Kurdish rebellions.

As Saddam predicted, the army was enthusiastic about their mission. He ordered his elite Republican Guard troops to brutally attack cities that were holy to the Shiites, such as Najaf and Karbala. Thousands of clerics were arrested and later executed. "Any turbaned or bearded man who took to the street ran the risk of being arrested and shot," notes one observer. "People were tied to tanks and used as human shields, while women and children were indiscriminately shot."[68]

Saddam unleashed that same brutality on the Kurdish rebels. Realizing they had no chance against the rapidly advancing Iraqi army, millions of Kurds fled into Turkey or Iran. Cut off from supplies of food in the most mountainous regions of the area, the Kurds were starving at the rate of nearly one thousand per day. To frighten the refugees further, Saddam demanded that warplanes fly low over the makeshift settlements and drop flour on the Kurds, who thought it was another chemical weapon.

## New UN Demands

The state of his economy concerned Saddam as much as the rebellion occurring within Iraq. He was already struggling because of the economic sanctions the United Nations had imposed earlier; Iraq was not able to sell its oil, nor could it buy the products it needed from other nations. After Desert Storm, however, there were additional demands made on Iraq that had to be met before sanctions were dropped.

First, Saddam was obligated to pay Kuwait for the damages incurred during the invasion. He was told, too, to provide the United Nations with a detailed list of all the illegal weapons Iraq possessed or was in the process of building, whether nuclear, chemical, or biological. The United Nations ordered that Saddam cooperate while a team of experts destroyed those weapons.

Saddam agreed to the demands, although he had no intention of complying with the Special Commission, the weapons inspection team from the United Nations. He planned to give them phony information, or move all traces of his forbidden weapons, until the inspectors were satisfied that he presented no threat. "The Special Commission is a temporary mea-

A man stares through the bars of an Iraqi jail. To regain control of Iraq after the Gulf War, Saddam Hussein ordered his army to arrest and execute his enemies.

sure," he assured his staff beforehand. "We will fool them and we will bribe them and the matter will be over in a few months."[69]

## Defying Orders

The Special Commission, which began their inspections in the spring of 1991, was given incorrect information by the Iraqi government. They asked to see weapons factories and plants where chemical weapons were made; however, Saddam informed them that those facilities had been bombed by the coalition army. However, the Special Commission was not as easily fooled as Saddam had predicted.

In June 1991, for example, the team visited facilities that Iraq claimed were only for research and for creating nuclear energy for homes and businesses. In truth, however, Saddam had instructed his son Qusay to find a way to conceal the equipment that would prove the facilities were for experimenting with nuclear weapons. According to biographer Con Coughlin,

In the course of inspecting the camp, [Special Commission team leader David] Kay discovered Iraqi soldiers attempting to move a number of huge electromagnetic isotope separators

# Difficulties with Weapons Inspectors

*The Special Commission of weapons inspectors insisted on being shown all of Iraq's weapons; however, Saddam's son Qusay worked very hard to make sure that most of the weapons were never seen, as Con Coughlin explains in his book* Saddam: King of Terror.

Qusay's concealment committee ordered that all the key components of Iraq's nuclear weapons programs be concealed at a network of Saddam's palaces and villas around Tikrit, which were not mentioned in Iraq's declared list of sites. Any material that was not regarded as essential was blown up by the Iraqis, who then informed the UN that they had unilaterally destroyed their nonconventional weapons, in the belief that the weapons inspectors would not return. Having already caught Saddam out once, the ... inspectors were not convinced. [David] Kay [the chief inspector] returned to Baghdad and in mid-September his team arrived unannounced at the Iraqi nuclear headquarters in Baghdad, scaled the fence, and burst into the building.

To their amazement they discovered millions of pages of documents detailing all of Iraq's nuclear weapons programs. Although Qusay's concealment committee had ordered that all the nuclear hardware be secured, they had forgotten about the documentation. Embarrassed Iraqi officials rushed to the compound, and a four-day standoff ensued, in which Kay's inspectors were virtually held captive in the parking lot.

... which were being transported on heavy tractor trailers. When Kay tried to intervene, the Iraqi soldiers reacted by firing shots over his head.[70]

For the next six years, weapons inspectors tried to work with Saddam to get more accurate information about his weapons—usually without success. Later, Iraqi experts would admit to hiding weapons and parts of assembly systems underground, in hospitals and in school buildings, and even on the grounds of Saddam's many palaces. Said one Iraqi official, "There were missiles hidden all over Iraq. I saw them stored under swimming pools and on farms."[71]

## "Disaster in Slow Motion"

The months went by, and still Saddam refused to meet UN demands. As a result, economic sanctions against Iraq stayed in place. Because Iraq was not permitted to sell its oil, it had little money to import food and other products people needed. Even machinery for water purification plants and farming could not be purchased under the sanction rules.

The result of Saddam's refusal, say observers, was that the Iraqi people were plunged into poverty and starvation on a massive scale. By July 1991, garbage collectors in Baghdad reported that they were finding that people were throwing away almost no scraps of food. Even the rinds of melons were being eaten, because there was so little to eat. The starvation was not limited to the poor. Hunger was so rampant that even middle-class families were among the mobs who flooded the street in front of the Catholic Relief agency that was distributing food.

One agency worker was speechless at the numbers of malnourished children he saw. He called it a "disaster in slow motion."[72] Although he said that he hoped he would be proved wrong, he predicted that as many as 175,000 Iraqi children could die because of the shortages resulting from the sanctions. In fact, the number was far larger: By 1995, after four years of sanctions, more than 570,000 children died in Iraq as a result of the shortages of food and medicine.

As stories of the suffering of the Iraqi people spread, the United Nations offered to help Saddam feed his people. In 1992, the United Nations told Saddam he could sell $1.6 billion worth of oil on the world market, with the understanding that the profits be used for food and medical supplies. Saddam rejected the plan, saying that he did not want to give control of Iraq's money to the United Nations or any other outsider.

Not everyone suffered because of sanctions, however. Experts estimate that as much as 70 percent of the donated medical supplies were appropriated by a growing number of Iraqis dealing in the black market, selling it for many times its original price. Uday was building a massive personal fortune by reselling the humanitarian aid packages sent by the United Nations. On at least one occasion, he intercepted shipments of baby formula and milk, changed the labels so no one would know it had been donated, and sold them at a greatly inflated price. Even when the United Nations eventually relaxed its sanctions in 1996, much of the food shipped to Iraq did not get to the people.

Saddam, too, found a way to circumvent the rules by setting up a secret system with which he could smuggle oil out of Iraq. According to biographer Con Coughlin, Saddam's security forces set up "a complex network of companies, middlemen, and smugglers that enabled him to sell large quantities of oil on the black market and use the proceeds to finance the regime."[73] The oil would be transported through northern Iraq and Turkey, and shipped out of Jordan's port of Aqaba. Within a year of the sanctions, Saddam's forces were moving fifty thousand barrels of oil each day. Saddam was growing even richer, while his people continued to starve.

## Uses for Illegal Funds

Almost none of the revenue reached the Iraqi people. Saddam used much of it to build up his military chest, by purchasing black market weapons from Russia, North Korea, and China. With billions of dollars

# Saddam's Mosque

Hoping to defuse some of the anger against his regime from the fundamentalist Shiite population, Saddam decided to prove that he was as devout as they were. In 1994, he announced that the largest mosque in the entire world would be built in Baghdad and would be called the Umm al-Maarik, which translates as "the Mother of all Battles Mosque"—a reference to his own description of Desert Storm.

The mosque was unveiled in April 2001. There are four thin towers, called minarets, on each corner of the huge blue and white mosque. Each minaret has been cast to resemble a Scud missile, the weapons used by Iraqi soldiers during Desert Storm. There are four additional minarets next to the dome of the mosque that are shaped like gigantic machine gun barrels.

Those who have seen the mosque say that the inside of the building is most unusual. Saddam commissioned an entire team of calligraphers and artists to create the mosque's copy of the Koran, the holy book of Islam. The 605-page book is written in ink made from Saddam's own blood. He acknowledged that over a period of three years, he donated blood for the book, a pint at a time. Saddam's press secretary explained that Saddam's purpose in making such a sacrifice was to show not only his devoutness to Islam, but to try to show that he is actually a descendant of the prophet Muhammad.

Muslims pray inside Saddam's mosque, the Umm al-Maarik.

flowing into Saddam's private accounts from the oil sales, it did not take him long to replace those weapons that had been found and destroyed by the Special Commission, or that had been lost during Desert Storm.

Saddam also lavished money on his security forces. A strong believer that money could buy loyalty, he created an elite new group which he called the Organization of Special Security, or OSS. Headed by his younger son Qusay, the OSS were handpicked as the bravest, most skilled fighters in Iraq. Not coincidentally, the vast majority of the young men were Tikritis.

Each OSS member was paid very well—about fifty times the salary of a doctor or university professor in Iraq. They lived with their families in the presidential compound and ate their meals in their own private restaurant. Saddam made certain that they had the best health care, sports facilities, and schools for their children. Twice a year, each man was rewarded with a new Mercedes. As one former Iraqi official notes, "They fear only God, and their God is Saddam Hussein. They were so powerful that even ministers called them 'sir' when they entered the Presidential Palace. No one took any liberties with them."[74]

## "Our Great Uncle"

Saddam continued to rule Iraq with an iron fist, however, so those who protested were killed. Many Iraqis who have escaped the country say that his regime became more cruel and more threatening than ever after Desert Storm. He had his security forces create an intricate web of observers and informants to alert the government when someone criticized Saddam or even made a joke about him. Any behavior that was seen as disrespectful of Saddam was punishable by death—even something as trivial as allowing coffee to spill on Saddam's picture in the newspaper. The Baath Party would dole out money to reward those who came forward with incriminating information about their friends, neighbors, or even their own family.

Saddam's cruelty even extended to his own family. In the summer of 1995, two of his sons-in-law fled Iraq, taking their families with them. They had grown weary of the brutality and the killing in Iraq, they said, and took refuge in nearby Jordan. When the men gave information to UN sources about Saddam's renewed programs to create and stockpile biological, chemical, and nuclear weapons, Saddam was furious.

In February 1996, Saddam telephoned the two men, promising them that if they returned to Iraq, he would give them a full presidential pardon. He held no grudges, he said, but he missed his daughters very much. The two finally agreed and made plans to return to Baghdad. However, they were met by Uday, who took the women and children in his car and instructed the two sons-in-law to go to Baghdad by themselves.

One witness says that when the men arrived at Saddam's palace, the president

Men tour the gallows at an Iraqi prison. After the Gulf War, even the most minor offenses became punishable by death.

was "drunk, red-eyed, and wild." Saddam accused the men of shaming the family and instructed his bodyguards, "You must remove this shame. You must get hold of them and cleanse this stain. Get rid of them."[75] The men were shot and their bodies loaded into a garbage truck and driven away.

## Paranoia

As he increased the amount of force necessary to create fear, Saddam was aware that his own life was in danger, too. He began taking extravagant precautions against being assassinated, hiring men who bore a striking resemblance to him as "doubles." When he left one of his enormous palaces, several of his doubles would leave, too. They all got in identical pearl-gray Mercedes and departed in different directions. No one except Saddam's driver knew for certain which car he was in, so the chances of an ambush were minimized.

Altogether, Saddam owned thirty-five palaces, twenty of which were fully staffed. To prevent an assassin from knowing beforehand at which palace Saddam would stay, each of the palace's staffs would prepare three full meals, as if he were actually there. His food was flown in fresh twice each week, and was sent to his team of nuclear scientists, who x-rayed the food and tested it for any dangerous substance.

When he worked at the presidential offices in Baghdad, Saddam always took precautions against being poisoned. "Before meeting any member of his government," explains biographer Con Coughlin, "Saddam would insist that they first wash their hands, a precaution against the possibility that they might have poison on their fingers that could rub off on a handshake."[76] Guests were routinely photographed, fingerprinted, scanned, and subjected to a full body cavity search, to prevent them from bringing in a weapon or explosives.

## Saddam and Terrorism

As the years went by without the UN inspection teams getting cooperation from Saddam, many nations of the world

## "The Tyrant Must Steal Sleep"

*Mark Bowden, in his article for the* Atlantic Monthly *entitled "Tales of the Tyrant," describes Saddam's gradual isolation and paranoia to the point that he can trust almost no one.*

The tyrant must steal sleep. He must vary the location and times. He never sleeps in his palaces. He moves from secret bed to secret bed. Sleep and a fixed routine are among the few luxuries denied him. It is too dangerous to be predictable, and whenever he shuts his eyes, the nation drifts. His iron grip slackens. Plots congeal in the shadows. For those hours he must trust someone, and nothing is more dangerous to the tyrant than trust.

Saddam Hussein … rises at about three in the morning. He sleeps only four or five hours a night. When he rises, he swims. All his palaces and homes have pools. Water is a symbol of wealth and power in a desert country like Iraq, and Saddam splashes it everywhere—fountains and pools, indoor streams and waterfalls. It is a theme in all his buildings. His pools are tended scrupulously and tested hourly, more to keep the temperature and the chlorine and pH levels comfortable than to detect some poison that might attack him …although that worry is always there, too.

He has a bad back, a slipped disk, and swimming helps. It also keeps him trim and fit. This satisfies his vanity, which is epic, but fitness is critical for other reasons. He is now 65, an old man, but because his power is grounded in fear, not affection, he cannot be seen to age.…So he works, he also dissembles. He dyes his gray hair black and avoids using his reading glasses in public. When he is to give a speech, his aides print it out in huge letters, just a few lines per page.

were frustrated. UN officials had been told by members of Saddam's government who had fled Iraq that he possessed as many—if not more—weapons of mass destruction as he had before Desert Storm. And if he did not yet have full nuclear capability he was very close to it. However, as sanctions were loosened somewhat and Iraq's economy improved, many believed that Saddam no longer had any reason to allow weapons inspections into the country.

The terrorist attacks on September 11, 2001, were a grim reminder of the hatred that some extremist Islamic organizations feel for the United States. Many U.S. intelligence officials worried that such groups may attack again, using weapons of mass destruction, such as those Saddam possessed, to attack the country or one of its allies.

Since Saddam had sworn revenge against the West for its support of Israel and its victory in Desert Storm, there were some experts who felt that there was a strong possibility that Saddam had supported the al-Qaeda terrorists of September 11. It is known, for example, that Mohamed Atta, one of the ringleaders of the terrorist attacks, met with Iraqi intelligence only months before the attacks—although there is no evidence that the meeting had anything to do with terrorism. In addition, Saddam had allowed al-Qaeda to set up terrorist camps in Iraq in the 1990s.

Saddam made no secret that he applauded the attacks. Though other nations of the world sent their condolences to America, Saddam cheered. "It is a black day in the history of America," he announced, "which is tasting the bitter defeat of its crimes."[77] To emphasize the respect he had for the mastermind of the attacks, Saddam proclaimed Osama bin Laden "Man of the Year, 2001." The following year, Saddam showed his support of other terrorists—the Palestinian suicide bombers—by sending cash rewards to their families.

## A Final Chance

Whether he was involved—either directly or indirectly—in al-Qaeda violence, Saddam was a key part of the terrorist threats in the world. Saddam's son Qusay praised his father publicly for making threats against the United States, and pledged his support for Saddam. In 2002, Qusay addressed his father in a formal speech to the government assembly:

> We know, and the brothers here all know that we have—with God's aid—every capability and ability. With a simple sign from you, we can make America's people sleepless and frightened to go out in the street. . . . We will prove to them that what happened in September is a picnic compared to the wrath of Saddam Hussein. They do not know Iraq, Iraq's leader, the men of Iraq, the children of Iraq.[78]

Aware of such threats, U.S. president George W. Bush pressed the frustrated

An Iraqi man stomps on a portrait of Saddam Hussein. When U.S. troops arrived in Baghdad in 2003, Iraqis began destroying the many symbols of Saddam's brutal reign.

United Nations not only to renew its efforts to disarm Saddam, but to request that Saddam give up power. Saddam had successfully evaded their efforts for many years, but it was time the United Nations backed up its warnings. Bush suggested another coalition force, much like the one in Desert Storm, attack Iraq if Saddam refused to step down.

Few nations were willing to stand with the United States, but Bush declared that the security of the world depended on Saddam's stepping down as president. With or without international support or assistance, the United States would attack Saddam, he said, if Iraq continued to ignore UN warnings. On March 20, 2003, after repeated warnings to Saddam and the people of Iraq, the United States and Britain launched a large air strike on Baghdad.

Acting on intelligence that Saddam was in a special bunker in southern Baghdad, the U.S.-led forces dropped four two-thousand-pound bunker-busting bombs where Saddam and at least one of his sons were staying in anticipation of the war. Shortly afterward, further intelligence indicated that Saddam and one of his sons were carried from the rubble on stretchers, but a few hours later Iraqi television aired a speech by Saddam.

## Dead or Alive

U.S. officials were dumbfounded, for they were certain their tip on Saddam's whereabouts had been accurate. "It was very specific," insisted a White House aide.

"This is where he is, this is where he's going, this is the possible location."[79] Experts studied the video of Saddam's speech and wondered if it had been taped before the attack. Others thought the speaker was not Saddam, but one of his doubles.

However, by the end of July 2003, no body had been recovered, and officials were conceding that Saddam was almost certainly still alive. Acknowledged former CIA chief Vince Cannistraro, "There is credible evidence that Saddam is still alive and being sheltered."[80] Officials explain that Saddam and his entourage simply move in with a private family, members of which are taken hostage so that no other family members tell anyone of Saddam's whereabouts. After spending a week or so at one house, hostages are returned and the family is paid thousands of dollars for the use of their home, as well as for their silence. On July 22, 2003, both Uday and Qusay were killed in a shootout with U.S. forces in Mosul—although there was no sign of Saddam himself.

No one is certain when the mystery will be solved. But whether he is in hiding in Iraq or has sought refuge in another country, many Iraqis feel that Saddam is still a danger. They insist that he has been on the brink of ruin before, but has always managed to keep control of the government with his iron fist. After a three-day visit to Iraq to assess the situation there, one U.S. senator says that people are frightened and believe

Saddam is still among them. "There's a basic climate of fear that is impeding the recovery, particularly in southern and central Iraq," she says. "There is a fear that he will return, that he will come back. And that fear prevents us from making progress as rapidly as we otherwise would."[81]

Until they see his body, few Iraqis are willing to believe that Saddam is really gone. His hold over the people, they admit, is very strong. For a grim reminder of his power, one need only to listen to the backhoes and shovels busy in the sandy soil throughout Iraq as they uncover more evidence of the crimes of his regime.

# NOTES

## Introduction:
## The Secret Graves

1. Quoted in Adnan R. Khan, "Killing Was Just a Game," *Maclean's*, June 2, 2003, p. 20.
2. Quoted in Paul Salopek, "Iraqis Unearthing Unmarked Graves on a Daily Basis," *Knight-Ridder/Tribune News Service*, May 8, 2003.

## Chapter One:
## "Son of the Alleys"

3. Quoted in Efraim Karsh and Inari Rautsi, *Saddam Hussein: A Political Biography*. New York: Free Press, 1991, p. 9.
4. Quoted in Con Coughlin, *Saddam: King of Terror*. New York: Ecco, 2002, p. 7.
5. Quoted in Sandra Mackey, *The Reckoning: Iraq and the Legacy of Saddam Hussein*. New York: W.W. Norton, 2002, p. 208.
6. Quoted in Coughlin, *Saddam*, p. 8.
7. Mackey, *The Reckoning*, p. 208.
8. Quoted in Karsh and Rautsi, *Saddam Hussein*, p. 9.
9. Quoted in Coughlin, *Saddam*, p. 13.
10. Quoted in Coughlin, *Saddam*, p. 16.

## Chapter Two:
## Saddam the Baathist

11. Coughlin, *Saddam*, p. 20.
12. Quoted in Elaine Sciolino, *The Outlaw State: Saddam Hussein's Quest for Power and the Gulf Crisis*. New York: John Wiley and Sons, 1991, p. 59.
13. Quoted in Coughlin, *Saddam*, p. 25.
14. Quoted in Coughlin, *Saddam*, p. 24.
15. Karsh and Rautsi, *Saddam Hussein*, p. 17.
16. Quoted in Sciolino, *The Outlaw State*, p. 59.
17. Quoted in Sciolino, *The Outlaw State*, p. 60.
18. Quoted in Coughlin, *Saddam*, p. 30.
19. Quoted in Andrew Cockburn and Patrick Cockburn, *Out of the Ashes: The Resurrection of Saddam Hussein*. New York: HarperCollins, 1999, p. 73.
20. Quoted in Sciolino, *The Outlaw State*, p. 61.

## Chapter Three:
## Saddam the Killer

21. Quoted in Adel Darwish and Gregory Alexander, *Unholy Babylon: The Secret History of Saddam's War*. New York: St. Martin's, 1991, p. 201.
22. Quoted in Judith Miller and Laurie Mylroie, *Saddam Hussein and the Crisis in the Gulf*. New York: Times Books, 1990, pp. 31–32.
23. Quoted in Coughlin, *Saddam*, p. 46.
24. Quoted in Coughlin, *Saddam*, p. 48.
25. Quoted in Darwish and Alexander, *Unholy Babylon*, p. 201.
26. Quoted in Darwish and Alexander,

*Unholy Babylon*, p. 201.

27. Quoted in Coughlin, *Saddam*, p. 67.
28. Quoted in Sciolino, *The Outlaw State*, p. 63.
29. Quoted in Coughlin, *Saddam*, p. 73.
30. Quoted in Karsh and Rautsi, *Saddam Hussein*, p. 55.
31. Quoted in Coughlin, *Saddam*, p. 152.
32. Quoted in Mark Bowden, "Tales of the Tyrant," *Atlantic Monthly*, May 2002, p. 35.

## Chapter Four: Saddam the President

33. Quoted in Bowden, "Tales of the Tyrant," p. 35.
34. Quoted in Coughlin, *Saddam*, p. 170.
35. Quoted in Sciolino, *The Outlaw State*, p. 55.
36. Quoted in Coughlin, *Saddam*, p. 172.
37. Sciolino, *The Outlaw State*, p. 66.
38. Quoted in Sciolino, *The Outlaw State*, p. 107.
39. Quoted in *America's Intelligence Wire*, "Terror Passed Down the Generations," May 8, 2003.
40. Coughlin, *Saddam*, p. 196.
41. Quoted in Sciolino, *The Outlaw State*, p. 112.
42. Quoted in Coughlin, *Saddam*, p. 197.
43. Quoted in Sciolino, *The Outlaw State*, p. 67.
44. Quoted in Sciolino, *The Outlaw State*, p. 120.

## Chapter Five: A New Path to War

45. Cockburn and Cockburn, *Out of the Ashes*, p. 82.
46. Quoted in Coughlin, *Saddam*, p. 233.
47. Quoted in Brian Bennett and Michael Weisskopf, "The Sum of Two Evils: Saddam's Nastiest Biological Weapons May Have Been His Sons Uday and Qusay," *Time*, June 2, 2003, p. 34.
48. Quoted in Jeffrey Goldberg, "The Great Terror," *New Yorker*, March 25, 2002, p. 52.
49. Quoted in Goldberg, "The Great Terror," p. 52.
50. Quoted in Goldberg, "The Great Terror," p. 52.
51. Quoted in Mackey, *The Reckoning*, p. 263.
52. Quoted in Miller and Mylroie, *Saddam Hussein and the Crisis in the Gulf*, p. 149.
53. Quoted in Miller and Mylroie, *Saddam Hussein and the Crisis in the Gulf*, p. 149.
54. Quoted in Mackey, *The Reckoning*, p. 279.
55. Quoted in Coughlin, *Saddam*, p. 251.
56. Quoted in Sciolino, *The Outlaw State*, p. 245.
57. Mackey, *The Reckoning*, p. 280.
58. Quoted in Mackey, *The Reckoning*, p. 280.
59. Quoted in Bowden, "Tales of the Tyrant," p. 52.
60. Bowden, "Tales of the Tyrant," p. 52.
61. Quoted in Karsh and Rautsi, *Saddam Hussein*, p. 245.
62. Quoted in Mackey, *The Reckoning*, p. 282.
63. Quoted in Coughlin, *Saddam*, p. 273.

## Chapter Six:
## Saddam Surviving

64. Mackey, *The Reckoning*, p. 300.

65. Sciolino, *The Outlaw State*, p. 264.

66. Quoted in Cockburn and Cockburn, *Out of the Ashes*, p. 13.

67. Quoted in Sciolino, *The Outlaw State*, p. 265.

68. Coughlin, *Saddam*, p. 280.

69. Quoted in Cockburn and Cockburn, *Out of the Ashes*, p. 96.

70. Coughlin, *Saddam*, p. 284.

71. Quoted in Coughlin, *Saddam*, p. 294.

72. Quoted in Cockburn and Cockburn, *Out of the Ashes*, p. 137.

73. Coughlin, *Saddam*, pp. 289–90.

74. Quoted in Coughlin, *Saddam*, p. 297.

75. Quoted in Coughlin, *Saddam*, p. 301.

76. Coughlin, *Saddam*, p. 297.

77. Quoted in Mackey, *The Reckoning*, p. 17.

78. Quoted in Coughlin, *Saddam*, p. 322.

79. Quoted in Romesh Ratnesar, "Awestruck," *Time*, March 31, 2003, p. 44.

80. Quoted in *United Press International*, "CIA Reported to Believe Saddam Is Alive," June 2, 2003.

81. Quoted in Amy Waldman, "U.S. Offers $25 Million Reward for Saddam Hussein," *StarTribune*, July 4, 2003, p. 1A.

# For Further Reading

## Books

Khidhir Hamza, *Saddam's Bombmaker: The Terrifying Inside Story of the Iraqi Nuclear and Biological Weapons Agenda.* New York: Scribner, 2000. Difficult reading, but excellent information on the way Saddam accumulated his weapons of mass destruction.

Laurie Mylroic, *Study of Revenge: The First World Trade Center Attack and Saddam Hussein's War Against America.* Washington, DC: AEI, 2001. Very thorough chronology of Saddam's support of the first act of terrorism against the World Trade Center. Helpful index and photographs help make this book usable by teen readers.

Don Nardo, *The War Against Iraq.* San Diego: Lucent Books, 2001. Good information about the causes of the first Gulf War, as well as a thorough index and bibliography.

David Schaffer, *The Iran-Iraq War.* San Diego: Lucent Books, 2003. Good information on the religious fundamentalism of the Middle East.

Rebecca Stefoff, *Saddam Hussein: Absolute Ruler of Iraq.* Brookfield, CT: Millbrook, 1995. Aimed at teen readers, this book has a good section on the history of Iraq.

## Websites

**BBC News** (www.news.bbc.co.uk). Exciting website detailing the history of Iraq, Saddam's rise to power, interviews with Iraqi people, and more. Search for "Conflict with Iraq."

**PBS** (www.pbs.org). This site has a great deal of information on Saddam's life and background, which is found on the web page "Frontline: Gunning for Saddam." There are very interesting interviews by some of Saddam's former aides, as well as analysis of the political situation in Iraq before the U.S.-led attacks on the country in 2003.

# Works Consulted

## Books

Andrew Cockburn and Patrick Cockburn, *Out of the Ashes: The Resurrection of Saddam Hussein.* New York: HarperCollins, 1999. Well written, with good section on UN sanctions and their effects in Iraq.

Con Coughlin, *Saddam: King of Terror.* New York: Ecco, 2002. Valuable information about Saddam's rise to power; very readable.

Adel Darwish and Gregory Alexander, *Unholy Babylon: The Secret History of Saddam's War.* New York: St. Martin's, 1991. Difficult reading, but helpful quotations.

Efraim Karsh and Inari Rautsi, *Saddam Hussein: A Political Biography.* New York: Free Press, 1991. Good section on the events leading up to the Iran-Iraq War.

Sandra Mackey, *The Reckoning: Iraq and the Legacy of Saddam Hussein.* New York: W.W. Norton, 2002. Very readable, with extensive bibliography and helpful index.

Judith Miller and Laurie Mylroie, *Saddam Hussein and the Crisis in the Gulf.* New York: Times Books, 1990. Good information on Saddam's childhood.

Turi Munthe, ed., *The Saddam Hussein Reader.* New York: Thunder Mouth, 2002. This is a helpful source, especially for one wanting to read Saddam's speeches and rare interviews. Unfortunately, this book does not contain an index.

Elaine Sciolino, *The Outlaw State: Saddam Hussein's Quest for Power and the Gulf Crisis.* New York: John Wiley and Sons, 1991. Very good section on Iraq's work to acquire weapons of mass destruction.

## Periodicals

*America's Intelligence Wire*, "Terror Passed Down the Generations," May 8, 2003.

Brian Bennett and Michael Weisskopf, "The Sum of Two Evils: Saddam's Nastiest Biological Weapons May Have Been His Sons Uday and Qusay," *Time*, June 2, 2003.

Mark Bowden, "Tales of the Tyrant," *Atlantic Monthly*, May 2002.

Jeffrey Goldberg, "The Great Terror," *New Yorker*, March 25, 2002.

Adnan R. Khan, "Killing Was Just a Game," *Maclean's*, June 2, 2003.

Romesh Ratnesar, "Awestruck," *Time*, March 31, 2003.

Paul Salopek, "Iraqis Unearthing Unmarked Graves on a Daily Basis," *Knight-Ridder/Tribune News Service*, May 8, 2003.

Marianne Szegedy-Maszak, "Tyranny of the Mind," *U.S. News & World Report*, May 12, 2003.

*United Press International*, "CIA Reported to Believe Saddam Is Alive," June 2, 2003.

Amy Waldman, "U.S. Offers $25 Million Reward for Saddam Hussein," *Star Tribune*, July 4, 2003.

# INDEX

Adnan, 15–16, 40
Aflaq, Michel, 27
Ali, 16
Arabs
    alliance of, with British, 17, 19
    Baathist views on, 21, 46
    birthday traditions for, 14
    countries inhabited by, 18, 22, 24, 57
    as threat to U.S., 65, 63
Arc de Triomphe, 57
Aref, Abdul, 34
army forces. *See* Iraqi army
artistic productions
    Baathist control of, 43–45
    looting of Kuwaiti, 64
assassination, of Saddam Hussein
    attempts of, 50–51
    fear of, 76–77
Atta, Mohammed, 78
Aziz, Tariq, 46

Baathist Party
    beliefs of, 20–21
    conflict of, with Qassem, 23–25
    following Persian Gulf War
        as more cruel and threatening, 75–76
        rebellion against, 69–71
    founders of, 20
    interrogation techniques of, 30–31, 34
    overthrow of military dictatorship by, 33–34
    purges of perceived enemies by, 36–39
    regime, postmilitary coup of
        protection of, 36–39
        strong start for, 34–35
    regime, post-Qassem coup of
        military overthrow of, 32–33
    regular army resistance to, 29–30, 32
    Saddam Hussein in
        as leader, 29–30, 33–35, 64
        as member, 20, 22–23, 25, 27
    secret police force of, 33, 35–36, 39
    split of, 32–34
    symbolic power of, 34–35
Babylon, 8
Baghdad
    Baathist politics in, 19–20, 29, 34

monarchy coup in, 23–24
    as nuclear weapons headquarters, 72
    secret graves found in, 8
    U.S. attack on, 79–80
Baghdad Military Academy, 16, 48
Bakr, Abu, 16
al-Bakr, Ahmad Hassan
    assassination of Qassem and, 28–29
    Baathist views of, 20–21
    Kazzar's plot against, 39
    plot to overthrow military dictatorship and, 33–34
    as president, 34, 37, 39–40
    as prime minister, 29, 32
    resignation of, 41
banners. *See* posters
Basra, 8, 68
bin Laden, Osama, 78
biological weapons
    in Persian Gulf War, 66–67
    UN demands for destroying, 70
    verification testimony on, 75
black market, 73, 75
"blooded," as honor, 23
Bodine, Barbara, 64
Bowden, Mark, 77
British government. *See* Great Britain
Bubiyan Island, 62–63
burial, Islamic law on, 11
Bush, George H.W., 69, 80

caliphs, 16
Cannistraro, Vince, 80
Catholic Relief agency, 73
"Chemical Ali," 59, 64
chemical weapons
    in attacks on Kurds, 59–62
    in Persian Gulf War, 66–67, 70
    UN demands for destroying, 70
    UN inspection difficulties with, 71–72, 77–78
    verification testimony on, 75
China, weapons from, 73
Christians, Baathist views on, 20–21
clerics, Hussein's terror against, 46–47, 70
coalition forces
    Bush's suggestion for, 80
    in Persian Gulf War, 64–68, 71

Cockburn, Andrew, 57
Cockburn, Patrick, 57
Committee of Free Prisoners, 9–10
Communist militia
    as Baathist enemies, 29–30
    in Mosul uprising, 24–25
    support Qassem's regime, 28–29
Communists, Baathist execution of, 38
conformity, 44
Coughlin, Con, 14, 26, 49, 59, 71–72, 77
coup
    against Baathist Party, 32–33
    against British monarchy, 23–24
    against Qassem
        attempted, 25–26
        successful, 28–29
"cradle of civilization," 16–17
credit (financial), for Iran-Iraq War, 53, 55–56
criticism, intolerance of, 36–38, 42, 51, 75

Dawa Party, 46–47
demonstrations, against Aref's government, 34
Desert Storm, 67, 80
    Iraqi status following, 68, 70, 74–76, 78
    *see also* Persian Gulf War
disfigurement, as control strategy, 45
dissent, intolerance of, 36–38, 42
donations, during Iran-Iraq War, 53
Dujail, 50

economics
    following Persian Gulf War
        as depressed, 68, 72–73
        illegal revenue sources and, 73, 75
    of Iran-Iraq War, 49, 53, 55–56
        offensive strategy for stabilizing, 62–63
economic sanctions, 64
    as "disaster in slow motion," 72–73
    loosening of, 70, 78
education
    Baathist programs for, 35, 75
    of Hussein, 15–16, 19, 27
Egypt, 20
electrical shock treatment, 31
employment, Iran-Iraq War impact on, 49
enemies
    intolerance of, 36–37
    silent, 36
espionage ring, Baathist execution of, 36–38
ethnicity
    Baathist beliefs on, 21
    in Iraq, 16, 18, 69–70

*see also specific sects*
Euphrates River, 16
Europe
    control of Middle East by, 20–21
    in Iran-Iraq War, 55, 62
executions
    following Persian Gulf War, 70–71, 75–76
    of government officials, 41–43, 46–47, 51, 70
    of Iraqi citizens
        by Baathist Party, 36–37
        by Kurds, 61, 70
        posting names and photos of, 9–10
        reasons for, 8–9, 70, 75
        secret files on, 8–10
        by Shiites, 46–47, 70
        as traitors, 38–39, 41–42
    of Kuwaitis, 64
    as Saddam Hussein's legacy, 8, 11, 42
exile, 27–29, 33, 59

Fahd (king of Saudi Arabia), 32
Faisal II (king of Iraq), 23–24, 30
false charges, 39
fear, 45, 81
financing, for Iran-Iraq War, 53, 55–56
food shortages, 69–70, 72–73
force, as political strategy, 19, 32–33
freedom, 56
Free Officers, 23–24
funerals, 49, 53

Geneva Convention, 62
Germany, assistance with chemical weapons by, 62
God, 65, 75, 78
government officials, 41–43, 46–47, 51, 75
Great Britain
    alliance of, with Arabs, 17, 19
    alliance of, with U.S., 80
    Iraqi rebellion against, 19, 21–24
Gulf War. *See* Persian Gulf War

al-Hakim, Sahab, 32
al-Hakim, Seyyed Muhsin, 39
Halabja, 61, 67
Hitler, Adolf, 62
holy war, 65
human shields, as military tactic, 66, 70
Hussein, Qusay
    concealment of weapons by, 71–72
    pledged support for his father, 78
    shootout with, 80
Hussein, Saddam

autobiographical film of, 26
birth date controversy of, 12, 14
bullet wound of, 25–27
bully tactics of, 27, 33
children of, 45, 56, 58–59, 71, 80
    as dead or alive, 80–81
    as deputy secretary-general, 33, 35, 39–40
early family life of, 12–15
as field marshal, 48–49
final chance of, to give up power, 80
as interrogator, 39–40
    techniques used by, 30–31, 33, 36, 46
Kazzar's plot against, 39
military aspirations of, 15–16, 19
relationship of, with al-Bakr
    political attachment of, 20–21, 32–33
    power and leadership images of, 39–41, 51
    takeover strategies of, 35–36, 39–40
on revolution, 38
as "son of the alleys," 14–15
sons-in-law betrayal of, 75–76
vanity of, 77
views of, on politics, 19–20, 33
wives of, 45, 58
Hussein, Sajida, 58–59
Hussein, Uday
    arrested for murder charges, 58–59
    exile of, 59
    negative attention from, 56, 58–59
    reselling UN aid packages by, 73
    role of, in regime, 75
    shootout with, 80

*ibn aziqa*, 14
al-Ibrahim, Hassan, 13–14
illegal weapons. *See* weapons of mass destruction
infrastructure, 68–69
intelligence officials, U.S.
    on Saddam Hussein's location, 80
    on terrorism, 78
Iran
    Khomeini's Shiite influence in, 46
    Kurds fleeing to, 70
    war declared on, 47–59
Iran-Iraq War
    cease-fire for, 49, 53–54
    death toll in, 49–50, 53
    declaration of, 47–48
    expense of, 49, 53, 55–56
    image propaganda for, 51–53
    ineffective operations during, 48–49, 51
    Iraq's monument for, 57

oil industry and, 49, 53, 62
public opinion on, 49–51
victory declaration for, 54
Iraq
    ancient history of, 16–17
    ethnic and religious groups of, 16, 18, 69–70
    power shifts in
        historical, 17–19
        modern, 28–30, 32–35
    rebellion of, against British, 19, 21–24
Iraqi army
    during Iran-Iraq War
        compensation following, 51–52
        effectiveness of, 48–49, 53
    during Persian Gulf War
        misled vulnerability of, 63–68
        reestablishing loyalty of, 70–71
    resistance of, to Baathist Party, 29–30, 32
Iraqis, purging of. *See* executions
Iraqi support, for Hussein
    following Iran War, 55–56, 59
    through terror, 41–43, 46–47, 51
Islamic Empire
    ancient history of, 11, 16–17
    changing hands of, 17–19
    looting finest art from, 64
Islamic extremists, 78
Islam religion. *See* Muslims
Israelis
    Baathist execution of, 36–38
    in Persian Gulf War, 78

Jajjo, Kamel Hanna, 58
Janabi, Abbas, 59
Jews. *See* Israelis
jihad, 65
jokes, intolerance of, 75
Jordan
    in Iran-Iraq War, 53, 56
    sons-in-law fleeing to, 75
journalists, 40–41

Karbala, 70
Kay, David, 71–72
Kazzar, Nadhim, 30, 39
Kemp, Geoffrey, 62
Khairallah
    rebellion against British and, 13, 19–20
    as role model, 12, 15–16, 19–20, 22–23
Khomeini, Ayatollah
    determination of, in war, 53–54
    as threat, 46–47, 62

killings. *See* executions; murder
Koran, 74
Kurds
    chemical weapons attacks on, 59–62
    in Iran-Iraq War, 59
    as Iraqi sect, 18, 21
    in Persian Gulf War, 67
Kuwait
    in Iran-Iraq War, 53, 55–56
    Iraqi invasion of
        coalition victory over, 67
        international resolutions for, 64
        military response to, 64–65
        offensive strategy for, 62–63
        payment of damages for, 70
        troop assembly and movement in, 63–64
        UN response to, 64–67
        U.S. response to, 62–64, 66
        victory strategy for, 65–67
    as "19th province of Iraq," 64

"Leader, The," 40–41
"Lesser of Two Evils, The," 61–62
Liberation Square, 36–37
literacy, 35
loans, for Iran-Iraq War, 53, 55–56
*Long Days, The* (film), 26
looting, 64

Mackey, Sandra, 68
al-Majid, Ali Hassan, 59, 61
martyrdom, 65
mass graves,
    discovered locations of, 8
    guarding of, with hypodermic needles, 10
    identifying people in, 9–10, 81
    as improper Islamic burial, 11
Matar, Fuad, 38
Mecca, 32
medical supplies, 68, 73
Mesopotamia, 16
Middle East
    historical power shifts in, 16–20
    in Iran-Iraq War, 46, 53–54, 62
    modern power shifts in, 28–30, 32–35
    in Persian Gulf War, 62–67
    political movements of, 20–21
military dictatorship, 32–33
military operations
    of Baathist Party, 28–30, 32, 34, 50
    childhood aspirations for, 15–16, 19, 48
    of Iran-Iraq War

        during, 48–49, 53
        following, 50
    of Persian Gulf War
        during, 63–67
        following, 68–70
    in 2003 against Iraq, 79–81
Miller, Judith, 28
minarets, 74
missiles, 66–67
    hiding of, 72
mosque, 74
Mosul, 80
    nationalist uprising in, 24–25
Muallah, Dr., 27
Muhammad, 16, 74
Munthe, Turi, 38, 65
murder
    political, 30–42
    professional, 22–23, 33–34
    *see also* executions
Muslims
    ancient history of, 11, 16
    Baathist views on, 20–21
    extremists hatred toward U.S., 78
    Hussein's sacrifice for, 74
    Hussein's terror against, 46–47
    in Iran-Iraq War, 46, 53–54
mustard gas, 61–62
Mylroie, Laurie, 28

Najaf, 32, 70
Nasser, Gamal Abdel, 20, 27
National Assembly, of Iraq, 51, 56
National Guard (Iraqi)
    as Baathist paramilitary wing, 32, 34, 50
    participation of, in Qassem coup, 28–30
nationalists
    in Middle East, 20
    uprising against Qassem and, 24–25
National Security Council, on Iran-Iraq War, 62
national security forces. *See* secret police
Nazism, 19, 65
nerve gas, 61–62
news conferences, 40
newspapers, 56
non-Arabs
    Baathist views on, 21, 24
    chemical weapons attacks on, 59–61
    in Iraqi sects, 16, 18, 57
nuclear weapons
    in Persian Gulf War, 66–67
    UN demands for destroying, 70

UN inspection difficulties with, 71–72, 77–78
verification testimony on, 75

oil industry
black market in, 73, 75
Persian Gulf War and, 62, 64, 70
OPEC summit, 40
Organization of Special Security (OSS), 75
Ottoman Empire, 17
Al-Ouja, 12–15
*Outlaw State: Saddam Hussein's Quest for Power and the Gulf Crisis, The* (Sciolino), 32, 47
*Out of the Ashes: The Resurrection of Saddam Hussein* (Cockburn and Cockburn), 57

Palace of the End, 30–31
Palestine, 65
people, as political problem, 33–34, 36
Persian Gulf
Iraq vs. Iran control of, 47–49, 53
Iraq vs. Kuwait control of, 62–67
Persian Gulf War
coalition victory in, 67
international resolutions for, 64
Iraqi rebellion following, 68–70
Iraqi troops invasion during, 63–64
Iraqi victory strategy for, 65–67
military response to, 64–65
offensive strategy leading to, 62–63
UN in, 65–67
sanctions imposed by, 64, 70, 72–73, 78
U.S. in, 62–64, 66
photographs, political use of, 41, 43–45, 47, 51
poets, Baathist control of, 43–45
poisoning, Hussein's fear of, 76–77
political movements, Baathists as part of, 19–22, 29
posters
defacing of, 68–69
political use of, 41, 43–45, 51–52
poverty
Baathist regime programs addressing, 35
following Iran-Iraq War, 62–63
following Persian Gulf War, 68–70, 73
power
of Baathist Party, 34–35
early images of, 39–41, 81
of revenge, 43
*see also* presidency
power expansion. *See* Iran-Iraq War; Persian Gulf War
presidency
economic impact of, 49, 53, 55–56
fall of, 8, 11, 79–80

following Iran War, 55–59
hero personality cult of, 43–45
in Iran-Iraq War, 46–55
ominous beginning of, 41–42
omnipresent strategies of, 45–46
paranoia and precautions of, 76–77
persecution of Kurds in, 59–62
in Persian Gulf War, 62–67
propaganda strategies of, 40–41, 43–45, 47, 51–53
public anger against, 49–51
special July 22 session, 41–43
surviving the Persian Gulf War, 68–77
terror against government officials by, 41–43, 46–47, 51
terror against Shiites by, 46–47
terrorism and, 77–81
worsening image by family and, 56, 58–59
propaganda, on bullet wound, 25–27

Qadissiya, 57
al-Qaeda, 78
Qassem, Abdul Karim
alliance of, with Soviet Union, 24
Baathist assassination of
attempted, 25–26
successful, 28–29
monarchy coup by, 23–24

Rafidain, Iraq as, 16
reading, control of, 56
religion
Baathist beliefs on, 21
as threat to Hussein, 39
Republican Guard, 50, 70
revenge, sworn against West, 78
Russia. *See* Soviet Union

*Saddam Hussein Reader, The* (Munthe), 38, 65
*Saddam Hussein the Crisis in the Gulf* (Miller and Mylroie), 28
Saddam International Airport, 43
*Saddam: King of Terror* (Coughlin), 14, 26, 59, 72
"Saddam Song, The" (poem), 44–45
al-Sadr, Baqir Muhammad, 46
Samurrai, Wafic, 66
San Remo peace conference, 19
Al-Sarraf, Ilham, 45
Saudi Arabia, 55–56
Sciolino, Elaine, 32, 45, 47
Scud missiles, 74
secret files, 8–10
secret graves. *See* mass graves

secret police
    control and loyalty of, 35–36, 39
    elite group of, 75
    post–Persian Gulf War activity of, 70, 73, 75–76
    post–Iran-Iraq War activity of, 50, 56
September 11, 2001, 78
shah, of Iran, 46
al-Shaikhly, Abdul Karim, 14
Shatt al-Arab River, 47
sheikhs, 17
Shiites
    Baathist execution of, 9, 38–39
    as Iraqi sect, 16, 18
    Khomeini's influence on, 46
    Saddam Hussein's terror against, 46–47, 70
    as threat to Sunnis, 38–39, 46
smuggling, 73, 75
songwriters, 43–45
Soviet Union
    black market military weapons from, 73
    Qassem's alliance with, 24
spies, 36–39
Stalin, Joseph, 33, 36
starvation, 69–70, 73
statues, defacing of, 68
strikes, against Aref's government, 34
Subha (mother), 13–14
Sunnis
    as Iraqi sect, 16, 18
    Shiites as threat to, 38–39, 46
Switzerland, Uday Hussein's exile to, 59
Syria, 27
Szegedy-Maszak, Marianne, 45

"Tales of the Tyrant" (Bowden), 77
terrorism
    coalition response to, 78–81
    against his own people, 41–43, 46–47, 51, 70, 75
    international, 43, 77–78
    al-Qaeda association with, 78
terrorist camps, in Iraq, 78
thievery, as family tradition, 12–14
Tigris River, 16, 68
Tikrit
    early life in, 12–13, 15
    later associations with, 51, 53
Tikritis

as Baathist secret police, 33, 36, 70
as Special Security recruits, 75
torture
    during childhood, 15, 27
    as legacy, 8–9, 11, 33
    techniques of, 30–31, 33, 36, 46
traitors, execution of, 36–39, 41–42
travel, control of, 56
treason, 27, 36
tribal leaders, 17
Turkey
    in Iran-Iraq War, 53
    Kurds fleeing to, 70
Turks, 16
"Tyranny of the Mind" (Szegedy-Maszak), 45

Umm al-Maarik, 74
UNESCO, literacy honor given by, 35
United Nations
    demands of, for destroying weapons of mass destruc-
        tion, 70–71
        final chance on, 78, 80
        inspection difficulties with, 71–72, 77–78
    humanitarian aid packages of, 73
    in Iran-Iraq War, 53–54
    in Persian Gulf War, 64–67
    position of, on U.S. attack on Baghdad, 80
United States
    attack of, on Baghdad, 79–80
    holy war against, 65
    in Iran-Iraq War, 55, 62
    in Persian Gulf War, 62–66
    revenge against, 43, 78

Warba Island, 62–63
waste management, 68–69, 73
water, as symbol, 77
water treatment facilities, 68, 73
weapons inspectors, difficulties presented to, 71–72,
    77–78
weapons of mass destruction
    following Persian Gulf War, 77–78
    in Persian Gulf War, 66–67
    UN demands for destroying, 70–71
    verification testimony on, 75, 78
We Came to Stay (motto), 34
World War I, 17, 19

# PICTURE CREDITS

# ABOUT THE AUTHOR

Gail B. Stewart received her undergraduate degree from Gustavas Adolphus College in St. Peter, Minnesota. She did her graduate work in English, linguistics, and curriculum study at the College of St. Thomas and the University of Minnesota. She taught English and reading for more than ten years.

She has written over ninety books for young people, including a series for Lucent Books called The Other America. She has written many books on historical topics such as World War I and the Warsaw ghetto.

Stewart and her husband live in Minneapolis with their three sons, Ted, Elliot, and Flynn; two dogs; and a cat. when she is not writing she enjoys reading, walking, and watching her sons play soccer.